# Modeling the Combined Terrorist-Narcotics Trafficker Threat to National Security

Alexander Woodcock and Samuel Musa

Center for Technology and National Security Policy
National Defense University

May 2012

The views expressed in this article are those of the authors and do not refl ect the official policy or position of the National Defense University, Department of Defense, or U.S. Government. All information and sources for this paper were drawn from unclassified materials.

**Alexander Woodcock** is currently Principal Operations Research Analyst at MITR E Corporation, a consultant to the National Defens e University, and an Affiliate Profes sor at the School of Public Policy, George Mason Univers ity. He is a Fellow of the Royal Society of Medicine, a foreign member of the Royal Swedish Academy of War Sciences, and a full member of Sigma Xi. He was a consultant to the Inst itute for Defense Analys es, the Naval Research Laboratory, and the intelligenc e community. He was also a Se nior Research Professor and Director of the Societal Dynam ics Research Center at the Sc hool of Public Policy, George Mason University. Dr. W oodcock was Chief Scient ist, Vice President, and Director of the Advanced Mathematics Program, BAE SYSTEMS-Portal Solutions (formerly Synectics Corporation), a Guest Professor at the Swed ish National Defence Co llege, and a Visiting Professor at The Royal Military C ollege of Science, England. He is the author of *Assessing Iraq's Future*, published by the Royal Swedish Academ y of War Sciences and co-editor with John Dockery of *The Military Landscape: Mathematical Models of Combat*. Dr. Woodcock has a PhD in biology and an MSc in biophysics from the University of East Anglia, England, and a BSc with Honours in physics from Exeter University, England. He was a Fulbright Fellow and Research Associate at Yale University, an IB M (World Trade) Postdoctoral Fellow at IBM Research, an IBM (UK) Postdoctoral Fellow at the University of Warwick Mathematics Institute, and a Visiting Scholar in Biology at Stanford University.

**Samuel Musa** is a Senior Research Fellow at the Ce nter for Technology and National Security Policy (CTNSP) of the National Defense University. He has held the Homeland Security Science and Technology Chair at CTNSP. He was previ ously Associate Vice President for Strategic Initiatives and Professor of electrical and com puter engineering at Northwestern University. He has served in various p ositions in academia, government, and industry, including University of Michigan, University of Penns ylvania, Institute for Defens e Analysis, and Offi ce of the Secretary of Defense. Dr. Musa s erved on th e Defense Intelligence Advisory Board, Arm y Science Board, and Air Force Scientific Advisory Board. He was Executive Secretary of Defense Science Board Summer Studies and Task Forces, and a m ember of the Scientific and Technical Intelligence Committee of the Director of Central Intelligence. Dr. Musa received his BA and BS degrees in Electrical Engineering from Rutgers University, and MS and PhD degrees in Applie d Physics from Harvard University.

## Acknowledgments

SM acknowledges the f unding support from the O ffice of University Program s, Science and Technology Directorate, Departm ent of Hom eland Security, and Office of Deputy Assistant Secretary for Defense (DASD) Counternarcotics/Global Threat (CN&GT).

# CONTENTS

# LIST OF FIGURES

iv

# MODELING THE COMBINED TERRORIST-NARCOTICS TRAFFICKER THREAT TO NATIONAL SECURITY

The relationship between terrorism, drug trafficking, and policymaking is examined through the development, implementation, and use of a series of system s dynamics-based models. These activities are intended to provide the basis for future developm ent of a decision aid to support policymakers in combating the narco-terror threat. The models developed for this purpose are: a narcotics, counter-narcotics, and trafficker double agent model; a policy cycle m odel to manage the trafficker double agent conversion policies; a prototype societal depr ivation, affection, disaffection, and advanced terro rist recruitment, training, a nd narco-terrorist support m odel; entity security and ter rorist activity models; a violence generation model; and policy cycle models to represent the management of social violence and entity security policies. These models illustrate the relationships between deprivation of key resour ces to individuals and disaffection and ultimate terrorist activity; attack of notional targets by team s of terro rists; deprivation of individuals leading to violence , which can lead to an increas e in the lev el of perceived deprivation; dynamics of policym aking in res ponse to perceived needs; and the im pact of corruption on policymaking.

The U.S. Federal Governm ent has well do cumented the strong ties between terrorist organizations and drug-trafficki ng organizations. A number of i ndictments are further proof of this relationship. In some cases, both organiza tions need the same facilitators: improve financial gains, expand geographical domains, provide common personnel protection, and utilize common logistical support. The U.S. ad ministration has released two im portant national strategies to counter each of these threats separately, al though their linkage is recognized. S ome policy considerations must be taken into account when both elem ents operate in the sam e theater, including the am ount of funds dedicated to combat these ope rations, the personnel resources required, and the level of intelligence gath ering and dissem ination necessary to produce meaningful results. Strategic a nd tactical considerat ions also m ust be acknowledged. On the strategic side, allocating resources to interrogation and "f lipping" of traffickers after their arrest can be productive in learning more about the entire network. On the tactical side, it may be more productive to devote resources to monitoring and det ection. In the case of terrorism, more resources directed toward radicalization, disaffec tion, and deprivation of i ndividuals may be just as productive as intelligence gathering and kinetic means of action.

This modeling study demonstrated that m odel-generated data closely resem bled actual reports about tons of disrupted narcotic s substances in thr ee consecutive years. The policy cycle m odel showed that increased rates of policy cycle activ ity increased the amount of narcotics disruption, while increased levels of corruption reduced those levels. Model-genera ted results show tha t policymaking can lead to a reduction in the leve l of deprivation, disaff ection, and violence and that policy-related effects can be inhibited by co rruption. The study also showed that availability of trained terrorists can be a rate-lim iting factor and that targets of opportunity may not be attacked because trained terrorists are lacking. Many more results can be generated depending on the assumptions used in the parameters of the models. These assumptions have to be validated by actual field data. These models can be enhanced to provide gui dance to the po licymaker and decisionmaker in selecting options for the allo cation of lim ited resources to support future counter-terror and counter-narcotics actions.

# INTRODUCTION

Interest in exam ining the rela tionship between drug cartels and terrorist organizations is increasing, as has been reflected in the recent congressional testimonies by leading authorities on the subject on July 7, 2011. [1] In particular, the Hezbollah gro up has been alleged to be working with the Mexican drug cartels to use existing dr ug pipelines to penetrat e the U.S. hom eland. In fact, research conducted by the American Enterpri se Institute for Public Policy Research has concluded that at least two para llel terrorist networks are growing in Latin Am erica. One is operated by Hezbollah, and another is managed by Qods operatives. These networks cooperate to carry out various crim inal activities, including narcotics sm uggling. The study concluded there are more than 80 operatives in at least 12 count ries throughout the region, and the regions of Brazil, Venezuela, and the Southern Cone are of the greatest concern. [2] Several reports address Hezbollah's financial ties to the contraband center of the Tri-Border region of Paraguay, Argentina, and Brazil, and the contributions of the Lebanese diaspora on Isle Margarita and other locations.[3] More recently, a new case, called Opera tion Red Coalition, began in May 2011 when an Iranian-American from Corpus Christi, Te xas, approached a U.S. Drug Enforcem ent Administration (DEA) inform ant. He was se eking the help of a Me xican drug cartel to assassinate the Saudi am bassador, according to counter-terrorism officials. The Iranian-American thought he was dealing with a m ember of the feared Zetas Mexican drug organization, according to agents; instead, the suspect was arrested on October 11, 2011.

Terrorist organizations are working with narco tics traffickers to in crease the m agnitude and extent of terrorist actions. Drug-trafficking organizations (DTO) in Colombia and Venezuela and the terrorist organization FARC, of Colombia, were indicted for moving cocaine through Liberia to Europe.[4] Considerable evidence indicates that FARC, operating on the Ecuadorian border, has developed ties to the S inaloa cartel, wh ich operates inside the Ecuadorian border. [5] Also well known is that West African criminal syndicates cooperate in illicit smuggling operations with Al Qaeda operatives in Islamic Maghreb (AQIM). DEA has confirm ed that 19 foreign terrorist organizations have ties with DTOs. Furtherm ore, Taliban ties to L atin American DTOs and Hezbollah have been well established. These are a few of the drug ter rorism alliances that have been reported in the literature.

The case of Hezbollah's ties to the drug car tels in Mexico is som ewhat controversial even with the mounting evidence from leading officials. So me experts think it is pure speculation that Hezbollah intends to launch terrorist operations ag ainst U.S. interests in the western hem isphere. One expert believes that Hezbollah is involved in mainstream Lebanese politics and has becom e more pragmatic and is less lik ely to confront the United States. [6] A closer exam ination of the Mexican DTOs suggests they ar e loosely organized with drug production based on dem and and distribution through independent pr oviders after point of entry to the United States. DTOs are

---

[1] US Congressional Subcommittee on Counterterrorism and Intelligence, House Committee on Homeland Security, United States Congress, Hezbollah in Latin America: Implications for U.S. Security, July 7, 2011.

[2] Testimony by Ambassador Roger Noriega before the Subcommittee.

[3] Testimony of Douglas Farah before the House Committee on Foreign Relations, Subcommittee on Oversight and Investigations, October 12, 2011.

[4] Douglas Farah, Terrorist-Criminal Pipelines and Criminalized States: Emerging Alliances for the 21st Century, *Prism*, Center for Complex Operations, Vol. 2, No. 3, June 2011.

[5] Ibid reference 3.

[6] Melani Cammett, Testimony before the Subcommittee on Counterterrorism and Intelligence, July 7, 2011.

family-based with ties to the land and community. Their strong religious affiliations and lack of interest in promoting terrorism differentiates their culture from that of Hezbollah. They certainly do not want to add visibility to their operations by being involved in terrorist acts. The main priority for such groups is making money. It is well known that the Lebanese communities in Mexico are wealthy but do not have any known ties to DTOs. The above evidence of partnerships between the cartels and terrorist organizations makes it clear that the goal is to generate profits for later use in recruiting, training, purchasing weapons, and carrying out terrorist attacks in selected regions. The groups use the same pipelines, exploit the same structures, and capitalize on the vulnerabilities of the population and legal system for mutual benefit.

Because of the growing importance of this threat, the U.S. administration has released two significant documents: the *National Strategy for Counterterrorism*, published in June 2011, and the *Strategy to Combat Transnational Organized Crime* (TCO), published in July 2011. Both of these publications address the terrorist and TCO threats separately, although linkage between the two is recognized. The latter document focuses on breaking the economic power of TCOs and protecting strategic markets and the U.S. financial system. It also seeks to build international consensus, multilateral cooperation, and public-private partnerships to defeat TCOs. The new capabilities created for this effort include a new executive order that establishes a sanctions program to block property and prohibit transactions. Another is a Presidential proclamation that denies transnational criminal aliens entry into the United States. A rewards program was also established to obtain TCO information, and the Interagency Threat Mitigation Working Group was initiated to identify threat and coordinate the means to combat TCOs.

This paper examines how terrorist activities might be supported by resources and facilities provided by narcotics traffickers. Of particular interest is determining how terrorist activities supported by narcotics traffickers might influence government policies and actions aimed at reducing threats and providing protection to the general population.

Trafficker-supported terrorist activities can corrupt the actions of the government by delaying the development and implementation of counter-terrorist policies and reducing their effect. This work builds on earlier research that described processes in which deprivation creates disaffection and creates the potential for violence. Disaffected individuals can be recruited into terrorist networks and trained to carry out terrorist actions within the wider society (Davis et al. 2003, Woodcock, 2003; also Woodcock and Cobb, 1994, and Woodcock and Dockery, 1989). Terrorist organizations can facilitate those activities and increase the scope and magnitude of their actions by working with narcotics trafficker entities. One of the main concerns is that terrorist organizations such as Hezbollah are providing technology for the highly sophisticated narco-tunnels being discovered along the U.S.-Mexican border. These tunnels resemble the ones along the Lebanese border and the Ghaza strip that Hezbollah used. The tunnels start inside the homes of recruited and disaffected families and end inside the homes of other disaffected families across the border. Detecting such tunnels by conventional means is very difficult. Extensive modeling efforts are needed to assess the impact of narcotic trafficker support to terrorist operations.

The estimated value of drug-trafficking operations is on the rise. The value of cocaine from South America to North America was estimated to be $38 billion in 2008 [7] and from South America to Europe, it was estimated to be $34 billion. Heroin traffic from West Asia to Europe was valued at $20 billion and from West Asia to Russia at $13 billion.[8] FARC in Colombia is the world's main cocaine producing organization. A highly decentralized narco-terrorist organization with extensive linkages to Hezbollah, FARC has more than 7,000 armed combatants operating out of the jungles on the borders with Ecuador and Venezuela. FARC has a strong relationship with high-ranking Venezuelan officials, including the president. The ties between Venezuela and Iran are becoming stronger and are designed to facilitate the funding of terrorist organizations. As for Mexico, the narcotics industry provides from $25 billion to $40 billion in profits from illicit drug sales. According to the U.S. Department of State, cartels and gangs employed 450,000 people in the cultivation, processing, and sale of illegal drugs, with one-third involved in processing and selling.[9]

It appears that both terrorist and drug-trafficking organizations need the same facilitators and leverage the relationship to mutual benefit. Other benefits of these partnerships include financial gains, geographic growth, personnel protection, and logistical support, but partnership-produced vulnerabilities include increased attention from law enforcement, potential compromise of internal security, risk of infiltration, and capture of leadership. A recent study [10] provided 10 case studies on the variations in the crime-terrorism nexus. These ranged from the full convergence/fusion of crime and terrorist organizations in the Dawood Ibrahim's 500-member D-Company operating in Pakistan, India, and the United Arab Emirates, to the terrorist organizations with in-house criminal structures such as FARC-based groups in Colombia, to the terrorist organization with criminal sympathizers such as Hezbollah. Other examples include the 2004 Madrid bombers, with decentralized terrorist cells having in-house criminal capabilities, and the Taliban with coalitions between terrorist groups and criminal organizations. The judicial system is almost nonexistent in West Africa, and the drug trade enjoys open sponsorship in Venezuela. As a result, the alliances between terrorist groups and criminal organizations will continue to grow.[11]

Some policy considerations may be relevant to the terrorism-crime/drug trafficking nexus. For example, how to prioritize the counter policies when both elements are present, as in the case in Afghanistan; the sharing of foreign aid funds to combat terrorism and crime; the role of the U.S. Department of Defense (DOD) in what has been considered a criminal justice and law enforcement responsibility; and following the crime-terrorism money trail.[12]

The above discussion makes it clear that narcotics traffickers and terrorists have distinct domains in which they operate. The narcotics domain consists of production and general assembly, primary and secondary transit systems, staging areas, disassembly, wholesale functions, and distribution for consumption. In each of these elements, the value of the drugs changes

[7] Robert Killebrew, Criminal Insurgencies in the Americas and Beyond, *Prism*, Center for Complex Operations, Vol 2, No 3, June 2011.

[8] Ibid, Reference 7.

[9] Ibid, Reference 7.

[10] John Rollins and Liana Sun Wyler, International Terrorism and Transnational Crime: Security Threats, U.S. Policy, and Considerations for Congress, Congressional Research Service, March 2010.

[11] Ibid, Reference 4.

[12] Ibid, Reference 7.

depending on the size, shipm ent, and location of the distribution centers. The value is highest during the transit stag e because of the size of the shipm ent. From a detection and monitoring perspective, this stage becomes the most significant. The terrorist domain is somewhat different. Certain precipitants can start the process, an d these include dissatisfaction, discrim ination, ideological beliefs, and so f orth. This leads to intern alizing values, possible indoctrination, following a charism atic leader, contact with a group, possible ideological seeking, and then committing an act of terror. This process of radicalization was discussed in a previous paper.[13] A definite profile for an individual ready to comm it terrorist acts no longer exists. Furtherm ore, the availability of the Internet is changing the process of radicalizat ion. The potential interaction of the narcotics trafficker and the te rrorist results from the need f or the same facilitators, financial gains, logistical support, and personnel protec tion as mentioned previously. Models that characterize the nature and degree of intera ction in the different dom ains is a useful consideration.

The role of law enforcem ent and policym akers in countering the drug traffickers and terrorists requires a more in-dep th analysis. In some cases, allocating resources to address the issues that lead to radicalization and terrorist acts can be productive. In others, providing resources to intelligence gathering and dissemination to the a ppropriate authorities ca n be m ore productive. The same can be said f or the role of the policym aker in the counter-drug-trafficking area. More attention to dealing with the stra tegic aspects of allocating resources to interrogation and the flipping of traffickers after their arrest can be quite productive in learning more about the entire network. In other cases, it can be productive to fo cus on detection and m onitoring for tactical reasons. It is then useful to consider policy cycle models to characterize the role of the policymakers in countering these threats, taking into account the number of factors that influence this process, including corruption of policymaking and policy-implementation activities.

## MODEL-BASED ANALYSES OF
## COUNTER-NARCOTICS ACTIVITIES

In order to address a num ber of the issues ra ised in the introduction, the narcotics, counter-narcotics process through the produ ction and use of seve ral models is e xamined in more deta il. These models will provide insight on the operations of the drug traffickers and m eans to counter their actions. Figure 1 o utlines the models that were develo ped; implemented in STELLA™ (a commercially available system s dynamics-based software system) by Woodcock;[14] and used to study the counter-narcotics and te rrorist problem. Two m ain activities were undertaken: (1) a study of counter-narcotics activities and the im pact of converting traffickers into double agents to disrupt narcotics shipm ents, and (2) an exam ination of the pos sible synergy of terrorist and trafficker activities, the impact of public po licy aimed at reducing violence and increasing counter-terrorist security levels, as well as the corruption of t hose processes by traffickers and other actions. Descriptions of the construction and use of the m odels are presented below. Implementation of the models is discussed in more detail in the appendices.

---

[13]  Samuel Musa and Samuel Bendett, Islamic Radicalization in the United States: New Trends and a Proposed Methodology for Disruption, Defense and Technology Paper 77, CTNSP, September 2010.

[14]  The models developed for the study described in this paper were developed by Woodcock using STELLA™, a commercially available software system (http://www.iseesystems.com). Details of the implemented software are presented in the appendices. Interested parties are invited to communicate with the authors for further information.

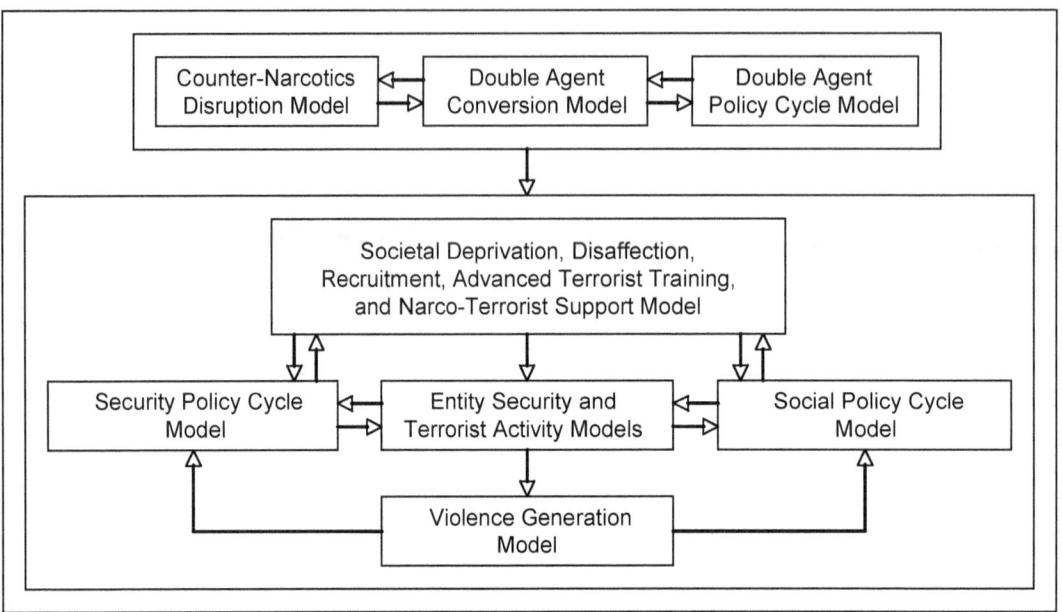

**Figure 1. Model-based analyses of counter-narcotics activities involved studies of the impact of creating double agents and of the possible synergy of terrorist and trafficker activities.**

- Counter-narcotics actions and the creation of double agents: This paper describes results of an investigation of counter-narco tics activities and th e impact of efforts aimed at converting traffickers into doubl e agents. Model-generated data closely resembled actual reports of tons of disrupt ed narcotics substances detected in 2008, 2009, and 2010. Success in counter-narco tics and trafficker conversion activities can have important public policy im plications. To examine those possibilities, a policy cycle model was developed and used to st udy the potential impact of increased levels of policymaking support as well as corruption of the policy process on the ability to form double agents and to disrupt trafficker activities. Increased rates of policy cycle activity increased the am ount of narcotics disruption while increased levels of corruption reduced such disruption.

- Examination of the possible synergy between narco-traffickers and terrorists and the impact of policy-related actions. In this paper, m odel-generated data show that policymaking can lead to a reductio n in the level of deprivation, disaffection, and violence and that policy-related effects can be i nhibited by c orruption, which can change the overall political dynam ics of societies of interest. Modeling the com bined terrorist-narcotics trafficker threat to national security has involved the production of several component m odels, including the following: (1) a *Societal Deprivation, Disaffection, Recruitment, Advanced Terrorist Training, and Narco-Terrorist Support Model* that illustrates how notional individuals deprived of key resources can becom e disaffected and recruited and trained to become advanced terrorists, (2) an *Entity Security and Terrorist Activity Model* that illustr ates teams of train ed terrorists attacking notional targets, (3) *Entity Security an d Violence Generation Models* that describe how deprived and di saffected individuals may become violent and how such violence can increase the level of percei ved deprivation and disaffection, and (4) *Social and Security Policy Cycle Models* that describe the processes of identifying a problem and for mulating, implementing, evaluating, changing, and/or term inating a policy in response to perceived need, as well as the impact of corruption in preventing successful policy-related outcomes.

## Building and Using a Prototype Narcotics, Counter-Narcotics, and Trafficker Double Agent Model[15]

A significant counter-narcotics strategy involves capturing narcot ics trafficker operatives and forcing them to "flip" or to give up information regarding their organization that could be used to reduce future trafficker activities. Such information could be used to create double agents whose activities might reduce the traffick ing of narcotics and reduce the ability of the traffickers to provide supplies to their clients. A prototyp e model has been developed and im plemented by Woodcock in STELLA™, a commercially available systems dynamics software system, to study the impact of those actio ns on trafficker capabil ities. Model-based studies show that increasing the effort to create double agen ts can lead to a corre sponding increase in the amount of seized narcotics substances. The model could serve as a basis for a more advanced m odel that captures additional components of the actions of counter-narcotics forces.

## A Narcotics, Counter-Narcotics, and Trafficker Double Agent Model[16]

The major components of the prototype *Narcotics, Counter-narcotics, and Trafficker Double Agent Model* are shown in Figure 2. Introductory sy stems dynamics-based modeling activities are presented in Appen dix 1. Selected details of the im plementation of the m odel in systems dynamics software are presented in Appendix 1 to increase the initial accessibility of the materials for the reader. In the model, a notional effort is assumed to take place that results in the transformation of narcotics traf fickers into ind ividuals that provide infor mation on trafficker activities. Traffickers that provide such info rmation can support counte r-narcotics efforts t o detect, capture, rem ove from the m arketplace, or otherwise disrupt the supply of narcotics substances.

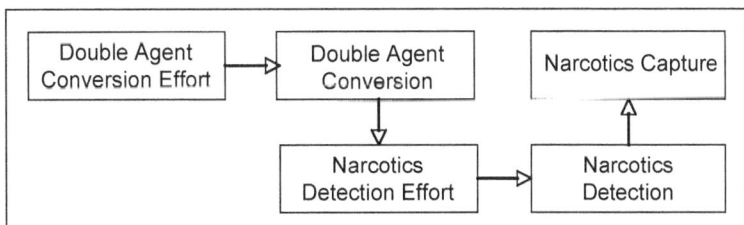

**Figure 2. A prototype model illustrates the processes involved in the conversion of traffickers to double agents and use of the information they provide to identify and capture or disrupt illicit narcotics products.**

The model was used to exam ine the effect of co nverting narcotics traffickers into double agents on the disruption of narcotics shipments. Results of those activities are presented belo w. In each case, the in itial threshold for detecting narcotics substances (represented by the param eter: *NarcoThresh* in the m odel [Appendix 1]) was assum ed to be 95 percent. This represented an

---

[15] The models developed for the study described in this paper were developed by Woodcock using STELLA™, a commercially available software system (http://www.iseesystems.com). Details of the implemented software are presented in the Appendix.

[16] Details of the implementation of this model are presented in Appendix 1.

assumed likelihood of detecting 5 percent of the act ual supply of narcotics substances. The model included a random number generator and a thresho ld device. Random numbers greater than the th reshold were considered to repres ent events in which narcotic s substances were captured or disrupted by counter-n arcotics activities. Thus, a threshold of 95 percent would lead to the capture or disruption of 5 percent of the total supply of narcotics. Each detected or disturbed narcotics event served as input to a second random number process that determined the size of individual shipm ents. A notional m aximum seizure size, represented by ( *MaxEvntSize*), of 100 tons was assum ed. In this case, disturbed or captured sh ipments were assumed to range from 0 to 100 tons of narcotics. A level of c ounter-narcotics effectiveness of using trafficker-provided information to increase the likelihood of det ecting or disrupting narcotics shipm ents, represented by ( *CN Efft*) of 0.1 (or a 10-percent effectiven ess of using trafficker-provided information) was also assumed.

| Conv Effrt | Total (tons) | Narcot Evnts | Doubl Agnts | Thresh Dep |
|------------|--------------|--------------|-------------|------------|
| 0 | 3376 | 68 | 0 | 0 |
| 5 | 6448 | 129 | 70 | 7 |
| 10 | 8881 | 173 | 142 | 14.2 |
| 15 | 10936 | 214 | 205 | 20.5 |
| 20 | 13263 | 260 | 275 | 27.5 |
| 25 | 16332 | 319 | 357 | 35.7 |
| 30 | 18990 | 373 | 427 | 42.7 |

**Figure 3. Impact of narcotics trafficker conversion efforts on the creation of trafficker double agents, represented by (*Conv Effrt)* and (*Doubl Agnts*), the disruption of narcotics shipments (*Narcot Evnts*), and the capture of illicit narcotic substances during a notional period of 360 days. Conversion of traffickers into double agents was assumed to reduce or depress the threshold for detection (*Thresh Dep*) and increase the likelihood of detecting or disrupting shipments of narcotics substances.**

The results of a series of preliminary studies of the im pact of diffe rent levels of effort aim ed at converting traffickers into double agents, with tra fficker conversion effort-related results ranging from 0 percent to 30 percent, are shown in Fi gure 3. Typical model-generated outputs are shown in Figure 4, which shows the control panel create d for the model, and Figure 5, which shows the number and size of narcotics seizures in the ab sence of counter-narcotic s intelligence efforts. Figures 4 and 5 and sim ilar figures are screenshots taken dire ctly from the STELLA™ output from the model.

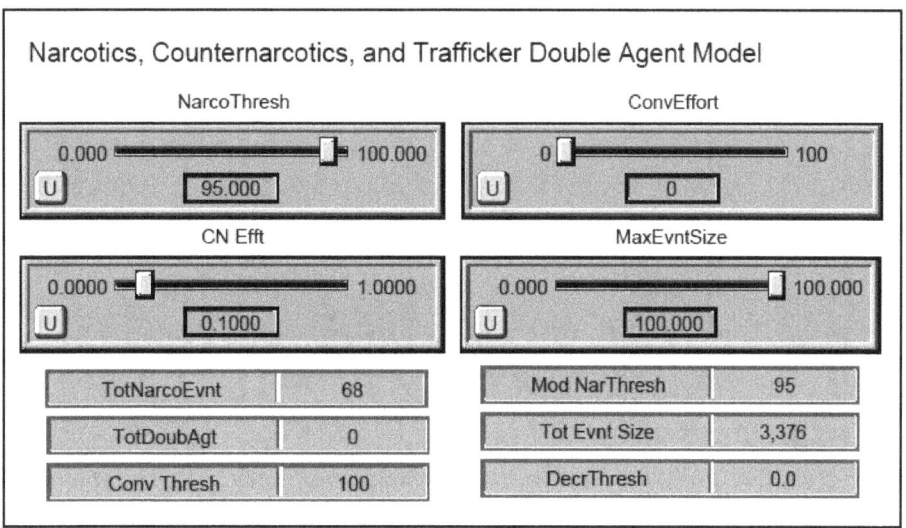

**Figure 4. Software slider entities permit user selection of model parameters and their use in studies and experiments. The model control panel shows that an initial threshold for detecting narcotics products of 95 percent and 0 percent trafficker conversion effort leads to 68 counter-narcotics events and the disturbance of 3,376 tons of narcotic shipments (*Tot Evnt Size*).**

In this case, the conversion of traffickers into double agents is assumed to increase the likelihood of detecting and disrupting narcotics shipm ents. This increased likel ihood of detection is reflected in a reduction or depression of the detection threshold in the model (*Thresh Dep*). Such a reduction would lead to the incr eased detection or disruption of narcotics substances. As an example, some 3,376 notional tons are seized in 68 counter-narcotic s events without the conversion of double agents, while 6,448 tons m ight be seized or disrupted with a 5-percent conversion effort involving 70 do uble agents and a m aximum shipment size of 100 tons. A conversion effort of 10 percen t generated 142 double agents an d 173 narcotics events that resulted in the disruption of 8,881 tons of narcotics. A double agent conversion effort of 30 percent generated 427 notional double agents a nd led to the disruption of 18,990 tons of narcotics in 373 events (Figure 3).

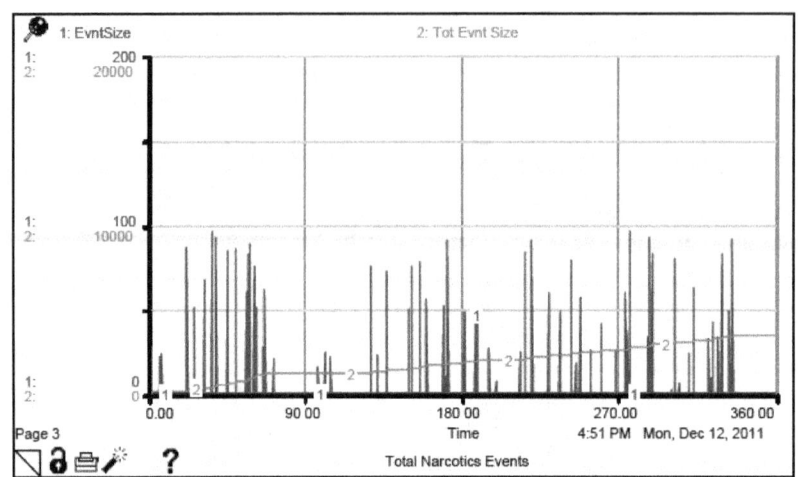

**Figure 5. Number and size of narcotics disruptions without counter-narcotics intelligence efforts. Some 3,376 tons are seized in 68 events during a notional 360-day time period.**

To summarize: Model-based studie s show that increasing the effo rt to create double agents can lead to a corresponding increase in the a mount of seized narcotics substances. The m odel represents the likelihood that a trafficker would be converted into a double agent and that narcotics substances might be detected, seized, or otherwise disrupted by a random process and associated threshold. Details of the im plementation of the model are presented in Appendix 1. Events are assumed to take place when a generated random num ber exceeds the threshold. The model could serve as the basis for a m ore advanced version that would capture additional components of the actions of counter-narcotics forces, includi ng details of the process of obtaining and using trafficker-related inform ation to increase the likelihood of detecting and seizing or otherwise disrupting the supply of narcotics substances.

Developing a more advanced model could involve validating the overall model-based processes and modifications that generate output data equivalent to actual fi eld-generated data. A preliminary comparison of model-generated a nd actual data of the disruption of counter-narcotics supplies is presented below.

## Modeling Actual Narcotics Capture Activities

An estimated 1,200 to 1,500 tons of cocaine are shipped from South Am erica to Central and North America on an annual basis. [17] Of that am ount, it is rep orted that the m ovement of some 264 tons were disrupted in 2008, 274 tons were disr upted in 2009, and 194 t ons were disrupted in 2010 (Figure 6). Those data can be used to determine model thresholds and to m odify the model described in Figure 3 and Appendix 1 to cal culate actual amounts of narcotics seizure or disruption.

---

[17] Private communication with Allen McKee, Joint Interagency Task Force-South (JIATF-S).

| Year | Narco Seized | % | Threshold | Total (2.0) | Total (1.9) | Total (1.8) |
|------|-------------|------|-----------|-------------|-------------|-------------|
| 2008 | 264 tons | 19.6 | 80.4 | 277 tons | 263 tons | 249 tons |
| 2009 | 274 tons | 20.3 | 79.7 | 291 tons | 276 tons | 262 tons |
| 2010 | 194 tons | 14.4 | 85.6 | 206 tons | 196 tons | 185 tons |

**Figure 6. Estimated cocaine shipments and actual cocaine seizures or disruptions (*Narco Seized*) can be used to set parameters for the random process model.**

With an estimated 1,200 to 1,500 tons of cocaine sh ipments from South America, it is assumed that the m ean annual shipm ent of cocaine was 1,350 tons. Of this total am ount, 264 tons represent 19.6 percent, 274 tons represent 20.3 percent, and 194 tons represent 14.4 percent. These percentages can be translated into thres holds for the random process m odel. Thus it is assumed that model thresholds should be set at 80.4 percent for 2008, 79.7 percent for 2009, and 85.6 percent for 2010. Such thresholds reflect the effectiveness of counter-narcotics operational efforts.

The actual amount of seizures or disruptions generated by the random process model depends on the assumed maximum size of the individual ship ments. Reportedly, shipments by airplane ma y range from 1 to 10 tons; shipm ents by "gofast" boat may be a maximum of 1 ton; shipm ents by fishing boat m ay be some 1.5 tons; and shipm ents by submersible m ay be up to 3 to 4 tons. [18] These values can be used with the m odel described in Appendix 1 to estimate the maximum size of narcotics shipments disrupted or seized by counter-narcotics forces.

Calculation of the a mount of di srupted narcotics shipm ents is essentially a two-stage process. The first stage calculates whether or not a disruption has taken place. The second stage calculates the size of the individual disrup tions. Addition of the individual disrupted shipm ents generates the total am ount of the disruptions. Threshol d values were set at 80.4 percent for 2008, 79.7 percent for 2009, and 85.6 percent for 2010. At the outset, the m odel-based maximum shipment size was set at 2.0 tons and without double agent-re lated activities. Model-generated data with that setting were 277, 291, and 206 tons for 2008, 2009, and 2010, respectively. W ith the maximum amount set at 1.9 tons, som e 263, 276, a nd 196 tons were generated by the m odel for 2008, 2009, and 2010, respectively. Lower total am ounts were generated when the m aximum amount was set at 1.8 (Figure 6). It is evident that the random process model with m aximum shipment size of 1.9 tons can generate m odel seizure or disruption amounts that are almost equal to the actual am ounts of those substances th at are disrupted. This success in replicating the amounts of seized or disrupted narcotics provides at least a measure of verification for the model. Additional research could be aimed at providing additional model verification.

## Policy Cycle Models Can Manage Trafficker Double Agent Conversion Policies[19]

The role of U.S. counter-narcotics policy on th e "flipping" procedure varies from increased allocation of agents involved in the interrogati on process, to advanced training, to increased funds to pa y the inform ants, and more. Modeling of some of these a ctivities can be useful i n identifying the major impact on the policymaking and the policy cycle. Processes involved in the development, implementation, use, and m odification of policies associated with a wide range of activities can be represented by an entity called the policy cy cle (Lester and Stewart, 2000; Woodcock and Falconer, 2012; and Woodcock, Chri stensson, and Dockery; 2006, for exam ple).

---

[18] Ibid, reference 13.
[19] Details of the implementation of this model are presented in Appendix 2.

Major features of the p olicy cycle are shown in Figure 7. Policy   cycle actions can  begin when problems arise in society and im pact existing gove rnment policies and activities. Thus, terrorist and drug-trafficking actions can create dem  ands  for  more  protective m easures  for the general population as these actions are reported in the media and discussed within the society.

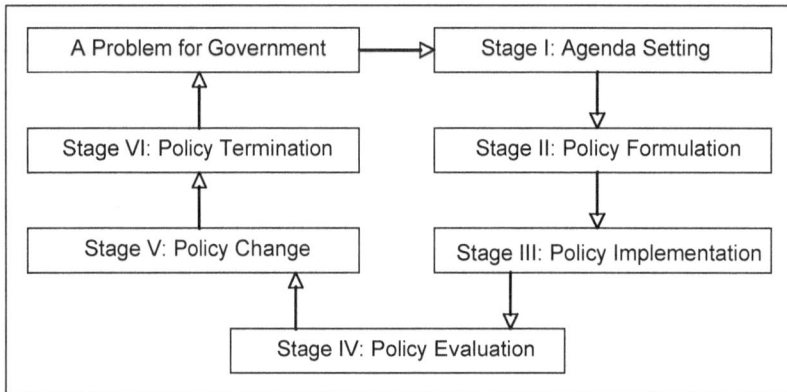

**Figure 7. Policy cycle actions identify a problem for a government; set an agenda; and formulate, implement, evaluate, change and/or terminate a policy to address identified problems (Modified after Lester and Stewart, 2000).**

Stage I of the policy cycle sets an agenda to ad dress problems and could involve discussions of the causes and effects o f the prob lems created by terrorist atta cks and narcotics trafficking and related actions. In Stage II, policies are formulated and legislation aimed at addressing identified terrorist and  narcotics  trafficker-related p roblems  is developed and passed. Such legislation might increase penalties for trafficker-and terrorist-related activities.

In Stage III, policy im plementation occurs and  can involve the definiti on and promulgation of new anti-terrorist or counter-narcotics laws and re gulations. In Stage IV, policy is evaluated and can involve assessing the effec   tiveness of anti-terrorist or c   ounter-narcotics  legislation in reducing access to d rugs. The results of such ev aluations can lead to policy changes in Stage V or to term ination of parts or  all existing po licies in Stag e VI. These a ctivities  can  create  new problems  that cou ld  lead  to setting   new agen das  and undertaking further actions to m   anage terrorist or drug-trafficking problems.

A policy cycle model of policies aimed at increasing the effort to convert traffickers into double agents has been developed and im plemented in systems dynamics software (Appendix 2). A key feature of this m odel  is the inclusion of prope   rties  that  reflect  the  impact  of corruption on undermining the counter-narcotics policy-related actions of a government. Corruption can inhibit the double agent recruitment process and reduce the amount of narcotics substances disturbed by counter-narcotics actions, for example.

Selected results obtained from the use of the double agent-related policy cycle model are shown in Figures 8, 9, and 10 and described below. Thos e studies used different settings of the policy cycle parameters: Input to double agent policy evaluation ( *DAgt Eval Inpt*), policy change (*DAgt Chnge Inpt*), and policy termination (*DAgt Term Inpt*); new policy form ation (*DAgt New Inpt*); and  the corruption of notional new policy (      *DAgt CorrRte NewPol*)  and for mulation  and implementation  activities  *(DAgt F&I Corrupt* ).  Those settings can refl ect different rates of policymaking and the effect of different levels of corruption on the development of new counter-narcotics policies involving the creation of double agents. Additional information is provided in Appendix 2.

- Establishing a perfor mance baseline: In creased conversion efforts increase the amount of disturbed substances (Figure 8) : A first study established a perform ance baseline for the com bined Narcotics, C ounter-narcotics, Trafficker Double Agent (Appendix 1, Figure A1.5) and policy cy cle models (Appendix 2, Figure A2.1) without policy cycle input. The ( *DAgt PolSens*) parameter was set at zero to prevent policy cycle input. The m aximum size of the narcotics shipments was set at 1.9 tons and the (*CN Efft*) parameter was set arbitrarily at 0.1. Model-generated results show that 263 tons were disturbed in the absen ce of actions that created double agents (Figure 10). Increasing the level of effort of trafficker co nversion to 5 percent, 10 percent, and 15 percent creates 70, 142, and 205 double agents and increases the amount of disturbed substances from 263 to 320, 371, and 410 tons, respectively. Levels of effort of 20 percent, 25 percent, and 30 percent result in the creation of 275, 357, and 427 double agents, and the disturbance of 445, 498, and 550 tons, respectively.

| Conv Effrt | Total (tons) | Doubl Agnts | CN Efft | Thresh Dep |
|---|---|---|---|---|
| 0 | 263 | 0 | 0.1 | 0 |
| 5 | 320 | 70 | 0.1 | 7 |
| 10 | 371 | 142 | 0.1 | 14.2 |
| 15 | 410 | 205 | 0.1 | 20.5 |
| 20 | 445 | 275 | 0.1 | 27.5 |
| 25 | 498 | 357 | 0.1 | 35.7 |
| 30 | 550 | 427 | 0.1 | 42.7 |

**Figure 8. Increased efforts (*Conv Effrt*) targeted at the creation of double agents (*Doubl Agnts*) with a counter-narcotics effort (*CN Efft*) of 0.1 increases the amount of disturbed notional narcotics substances due to a reduction of the threshold level for triggering disturbances (*Thresh Dep*).**

- Increased policy cycle-related inform ation transfer rates without corruption can increase the amount of disturbed substances (Figure 9): An established perform ance baseline (Figure 8) provides a basis for a study of the impact of different rates of transfer of notional information within th e policy cycle model in th e absence of notional corruption (Appendix 2, F igure A2.1). The influence of corruption was prevented by setting the corruption of new policy ( *DAgt CorrRte NewPol*) and the corruption of for mulation and implem entation process (*DAgt F&I Corrupt)* parameters equal to zero. Increasing the po licy cycle parameters of policy evaluation (*DAgt Eval Inpt*), policy change ( *DAgt Chnge Inpt*), policy termination (*DAgt Term Inpt*), and new policy ( *DAgt New Inpt*) from 0 to 0.1 (10 percent per tim e step) increased the amount of disturbed narcotics substances from 320 tons to 369 tons; the number of double agent conversions increased from 70 to 180.

13

| PCM Param | Total (Tons) | Doubl Agnts | Thresh Dep |
|---|---|---|---|
| 0 | 320 | 70 | 7 |
| 0.02 | 341 | 133 | 13.3 |
| 0.04 | 354 | 160 | 16 |
| 0.06 | 358 | 169 | 16.9 |
| 0.08 | 368 | 177 | 17.7 |
| 0.1 | 369 | 180 | 18 |

**Figure 9. Increased rates of policy cycle parameter (*PCM Param*) information transfer from 0 to 0.1 (0 to 10 percent per time step) increase the amount of disturbed narcotics shipments and number of converted double agents (*Doubl Agnts*) caused by depression of the threshold for detection (*Thresh Dep*).**

- Policy cycle-related corruption decreases th e amount of disturbed substances (Figure 10): A third study demonstrated that increased     levels of corruption can offset the impact of increased policy cycle inform ation transfer rates, reducing the a mount of disturbed narcotics shipments and the num ber of double agents. Thus som e 369 tons of  narcotics substances can be distur    bed and 180 double agents can be created without corruption. By contrast, 327 tons can  be disturbed and 78 agents created with a corruption level of 0.05 (5 percent per time step).

| Corrupt Lvl | Total (Tons) | Doubl Agnts | Thresh Dep |
|---|---|---|---|
| 0 | 369 | 180 | 18 |
| 0.01 | 339 | 111 | 11.1 |
| 0.02 | 331 | 91 | 9.1 |
| 0.03 | 330 | 84 | 8.4 |
| 0.04 | 327 | 78 | 7.8 |
| 0.05 | 327 | 78 | 7.8 |

**Figure 10. Increased levels of corruption (*Corrupt Lvl*) can offset the impact of increased policy information transfer rates, reducing the amount of disturbed narcotics shipments and the number of double agents (*Doubl Agnts*).**

The  studies reported above have    shown  that notional increased    efforts  involving creation of double  agents  can in crease  the am ount  of dis turbed  notional  narcotics  substances.  Additional studies  have  illustrated  the notional im     pact  of policymaking on c    ounter-narcotics  efforts involving the creation of double agen ts. Increased rates of policy inform ation transfer increase the amount of disturbed narcotics shipm ents and the number of converted double agents. A third study demonstrated that increased levels of corr uption can offset the impact of increased policy information  transfer rates and reduce the am     ount  of disturbed narcotics shipm  ents  and  the number  of converted double agents. These results      suggest that further investigation of the process of double agent formation and the role of policymaking might be pursued with benefit.

The  studies were continued to   investigate  the possible  impact of a synergy between narcotics traffickers on the one hand and terrorist and insurgent entities on the other.

## Building and Using Combined Terrorist-Narcotics Trafficker Models

Modeling the combined terrorist-narcotics trafficker threat to national security has involved the development and im plementation in system s dynamics software of several com ponent models (Figure 11). Production and use of  those models in a series of st udies are described. The overall model consists of the following major functional components.

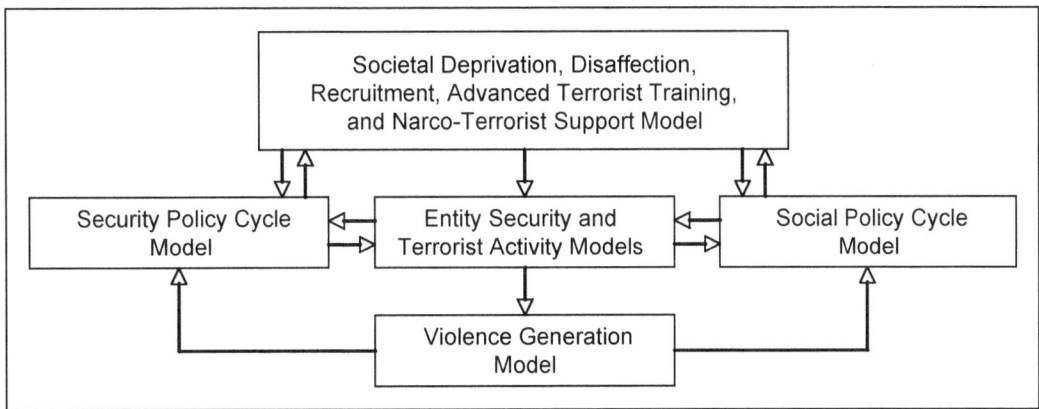

**Figure 11. Insights gained from modeling the combined terrorist-narcotics trafficker threat to national security can provide guidance to policymakers and decisionmakers.**

- A Societal Deprivation, Disaffection, Recruitment, Advanced Terrorist Training, and Narco-Terrorist Support Model illustrates how notional individuals deprived of key resources can becom e disaffected, recrui ted, and trained to becom e advanced terrorists. Terrorist activities can be s upported by narcotics trafficker personnel and resources and can lead to increased violence and casualties within an overall society.

- An Entity Security and Terrorist Activity Model illustrates teams of trained terrorists attacking notional targets. A ttacks take place when targets are sufficiently vulnerable and sufficient trained terrorists are available. Model-generated data provide estim ates of the number of casualties caused by terroris t attacks as well as te rrorist losses from those activities.

- A Violence Generation Model describes how deprived an d disaffected individuals may become violent and how suc h violence can increas e the leve l of perceived deprivation and disaffection. Policy-related actions by notional government entities can act to reduce the level of disaffection and the corresponding level of violence.

- Security and Social Po licy Cycle Models describe the processes of identifying a problem and for mulating, implementing, evaluating, changing, and/or term inating a policy in response to percei ved need. Policy Cycle m odels have been developed to permit changes in policies that increase security and reduce deprivation by increasing satisfaction and reducing violence levels, respectively. A novel feature added to the Policy Cycle models is the im pact of corruption on the policym aking processes that can reduce overall policym aking effectiveness and prevent lowering of violence levels, for example.

## A Societal Deprivation, Affection, Disaffection, Advanced Terrorist Recruitment, Training, and Narco-Terrorist Support Model[20]

A prototype *Societal Deprivation, Affe ction, Disaffection, Advan ced Terrorist Recruitment Training, and Narco-Terrorist Support Model* has been developed and implem ented in systems dynamics software (Figure 12 and A ppendix 3). The model represents the action of two basic processes assumed to be involved in the producti on and fielding of terrorist assets. One process

---

[20] Details of the implementation of this model are presented in Appendix 3.

involves the recruitment and training of disaffected individuals from the wider society to provide terrorist operatives. The second process involves the recruitm ent and advanced training of individuals provided by narcotics trafficker organizations. Those trafficker organizations are also assumed to provide resources that could support training and other operati onally related actions. They are also assum ed to provide resources to corrup t and redu ce the effectiven ess of government policymaking and other activities aimed at reducing disaffection and violence levels and stabilizing an overall society.

Major features of the Affection, Disaffectio n Terrorist Recruitm ent, Training, and Narco-Terrorist Support Model are shown in Figure 12. The implemented model is shown in Appendix 3, Figure A3.1, and the model control panel is shown in Appendix 3, Figure A3.2. The violence, casualties, and other deprivations caused by terrorist actions are assumed to disaffect individuals who were previous ly affected to ward a gov ernment entity. Governm ent actions aim ed at satisfying deprivations can transfor m disaffected into affected i ndividuals. Disaffected individuals can be recruited by terrorist organizations and m ay undergo som e form of basi c terrorist-related training. Basic training could be followed by m ore advanced training aim ed at providing operationally com petent terrorists. The m odel has facilities representing the recruitment of narcotics trafficker personnel in to the advanced training activities. Following advanced training, the individual s would be available to undert ake terrorist ope rations. Such operations have been modeled as described in th e Entity Security and Terrorist Activity Models section of this paper.

Selected output levels of basically trained a nd advanced terrorists are shown in Figure 13 and Appendix 3, Figure A 3.2. An initial popula tion of 100,000 individuals and 200 personnel provided by narcotics traffickers w as assumed. Levels of deprivation and satisfaction for a particular setting of model param eters created 84,798 affected and 13,208 disaffected individuals. After the passage of a notional 300-day period, som e 574 basic terrorists and 37 advanced terrorists were generated by the modeled training and te rrorist event processes (Figure 13). The "stair-step" nature of the output of tr ained terrorist personnel reflects the assum ed size of the trainee terrorist cohorts and training duration in the m odel. Training throughput can be increased by increasing capacity and reducing th e time needed for training. It was envisioned that trafficker resources m ight support increased advanced terrorist tr aining capacity, and this might be examined in future model-based studies.

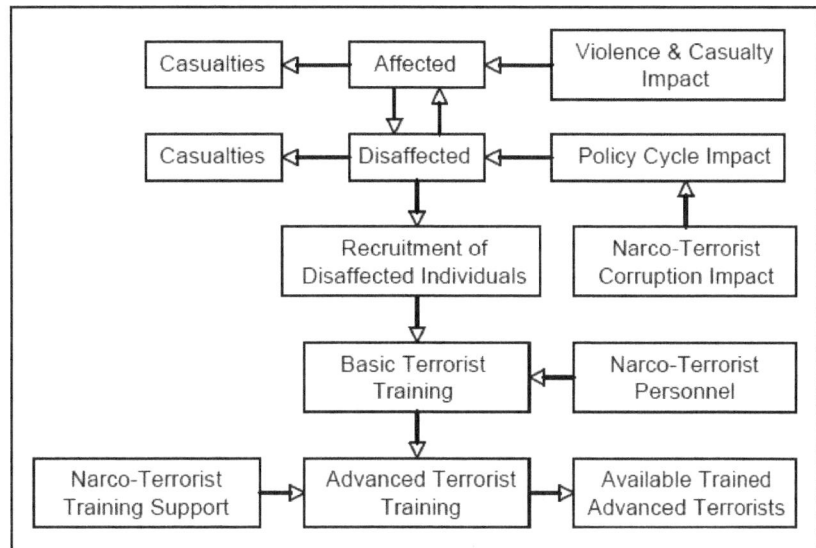

**Figure 12. Key activities of the Societal Deprivation, Affection, Disaffection, Advanced Terrorist Recruitment, Training, and Narco-Terrorist Support Model generate notional trained terrorists who are available to undertake terrorist activities.**

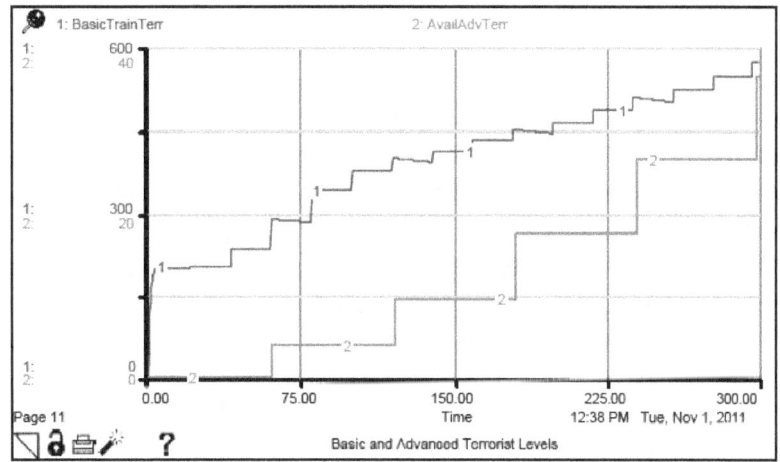

**Figure 13. Model-generated numbers of notional basic and advanced terrorists. In this particular case some 574 basic terrorists and 37 advanced terrorists were produced.**

An additional study investigated the impact of different numbers of trafficker-provided basically trained terrorists on the availability for operations of terrorists with advanced training. Selected results are presented in Figure 14. With a recruitment rate for advanced terrorist training of 0.001 (0.01 percent per tim e step) som e 200 trafficker recruits can provide 181 basically trained terrorists and 19 terrorists with advanced training after a noti onal period of 300 tim e steps. A combination of trafficker-supplied personnel and di saffected individuals r ecruited at a rate of 0.0001 (0.01 percent of availabl e personnel per tim e step) can provide 326 basic and 28 advanced terrorists after 300 notional days, for example.

| Traff Staff | Basic Terr | Adv Terr |
|:-----------:|:----------:|:--------:|
| 50 | 45 | 5 |
| 100 | 90 | 9 |
| 150 | 136 | 14 |
| 200 | 181 | 19 |

| Recrt Rte | Basic Terr | Adv Terr |
|:---------:|:----------:|:--------:|
| 0 | 181 | 19 |
| 0.0001 | 326 | 28 |
| 0.0005 | 883 | 62 |
| 0.001 | 1579 | 77 |

**Figure 14. (a) Trafficker-supplied (*Traff Staff*) personnel can train to become terrorists with basic (*Basic Terr*) and advanced (*Adv Terr*) training and (b) Trafficker supplied personnel can be combined with disaffected individuals recruited from the general population (*Recrt Rte*) to provide terrorists with basic and advanced training.**

## Entity Security and Terrorist Activity Models[21]

*Prototype Entity Security and Terrorist Activity Models* have been produced to represent the impact of model-generated numbers of basic and advanced terrorists and the level of security of notional target entities on terrorist activity outcomes. Major functional features of the models are shown in Figure 15. Implementation of the models is illustrated in Appendix 4, Figure A4.1. Reduced security and increased recruitment rates can increase the number of terrorist events.

The *Entity Security Model* component represents the level of security associated with notional target entities. Security investments can increase the level of security and security losses can reduce the level of security from user-selected initial conditions. Security levels can also be increased as a result of the implementation of new security policy actions triggered by losses caused by policy cycle-related terrorist actions, as described below. The level of new policy activity is calculated by the security policy cycle model components.

The *Terrorist Activity Model* component generates notional terrorist events. Those events, referred to as potential terrorist events, are possible when the notional security level falls below a number that has been randomly generated by the model. However, such events may not take place if sufficient terrorists with advanced training are not available. Actual terrorist events take place when sufficient terrorists with advanced training are available and the level of security falls below the generated random number. Security assessments are generated by the model and represent the likelihood that notional entities might be subject to a terrorist attack.

---

[21] Details of the implementation of these models are presented in Appendix 4.

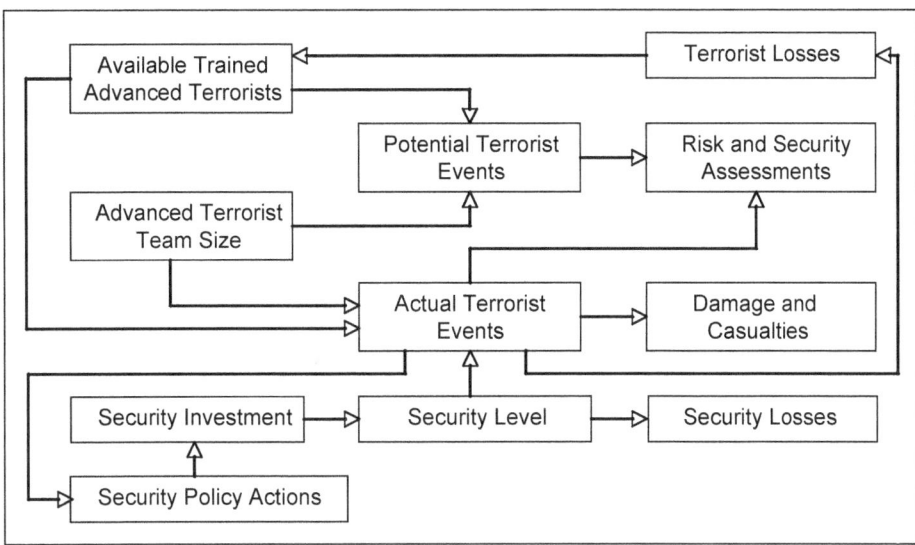

**Figure 15. Entity Security and Terrorist Activity models calculate the level of security based on security investment and losses. Security investment levels can be increased as a result of government policy actions. Terrorist events can take place when adequate advanced trained terrorists are available and the security level is sufficiently low.**

| Team Size | Terr Evnts | Tot Casults | Terrst Loss |
|-----------|------------|-------------|-------------|
| 1 | 26 | 1396 | 26 |
| 2 | 13 | 727 | 26 |
| 3 | 9 | 418 | 27 |
| 4 | 7 | 342 | 28 |
| 5 | 6 | 290 | 30 |
| 6 | 5 | 281 | 30 |

**Figure 16. Increasing the terrorist team size (*Team Size*) reduces the total number of actual terrorist events (*Terr Evnts*) because of staffing considerations. Smaller teams can become involved in a larger number of events and may generate more total casualties (*Tot Casults*) and fewer terrorist losses (*Terrst Loss*). Selected output from the Entity Security and Terrorist Activity Models with a security investment of 0 percent per time step, an initial security level of 100, and security loss rate of 0.0004 (0.04 percent) are shown.**

The Control Panel for the Entity Security and Terrorist Activity Models is presented in Appendix 4, Figure A4.2. Selected model output data involving teams formed from one to six members are presented in Figure 16. Inspection of the m odel-generated output suggests that terrorist actions may not take place under some circumstances because suitably trained individuals to fulfill team size requirements may not be available, for exampl e. As a result, care should be exercised when attempting to identify cause-and-effect relationships. Model-generated data for particular settings show that terrorist team s consisting of a single individual create co nditions in which m ore terrorist events can be undertaken com pared with situations involving larger team s because personnel are available. In a particular use of th e model, the initial security level was set at 100 units and declin ed to 88.7 after 300 tim e units due to losses of security, perhaps because of terrorist actions and lack of concern of securi ty personnel. Model-generated data show that terrorist teams consisting of one member might undertake 26 terrorist events and create 1,396 notional casualties with an assumed loss of 26 terrorists. Teams of six terrorists could be involved in five events and create some 281 casualties with the assumed loss in action of 30 terrorists, for example (Figure 16).

## A Violence Generation Model[22]

The prototype *Violence Generation Model* calculates the notional level of violence generated in response to societal deprivation, disaffection, and other factors. The major features of the Violence Generation Model are illustrated in Figure 17. Implementation of the model in systems dynamics software is shown in Appendix 5, Figure A5.1. The model control panel is presented in Appendix 5, Figure A 5.2. Deprivation is assumed to transform affected individuals into disaffected individuals. Satisfaction of needs, perhaps due to government and other entity actions, is assumed to transform disaffected into affected individuals. Deprivation and satisfaction are assumed to take place at user-selected rates. Relatively high rates of deprivation can create increased levels of disaffection.

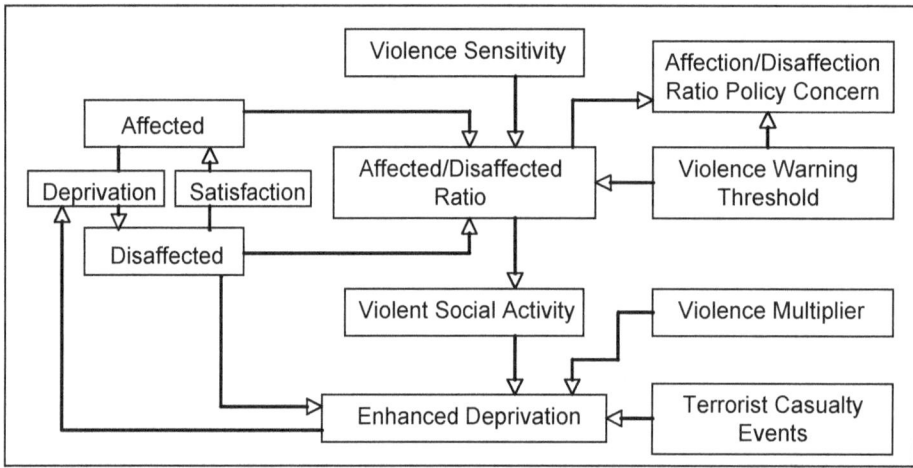

**Figure 17. The Violence Generation Model calculates the level of violence based on notional levels of disaffection and affection caused by deprivation and satisfaction, respectively, and social violence sensitivity, reflected in the violence warning threshold parameter. Feelings of insecurity and threat as a result of violence and terrorist-related casualties, for example, can cause enhanced deprivation.**

Sample model-generated output is presented in Figure 18. In this case, randomly generated violent activity (*Violence*) and *AD Concern* outputs are produced when the ratio (*Disaffected/(Affected + Disaffected)*) rises above the *AD POL Warn* threshold. That threshold was assumed to represent the historical experience of a country of interest. Violence in countries with a history of violence is more likely to occur at relatively lower disaffection levels, for example. The *AD Concern* model-generated output triggers activities that generate instructions for creating a new policy (*Soc New Pol*), as described below and in Appendix 6.

---

[22] Details of the implementation of this model are presented in Appendix 5.

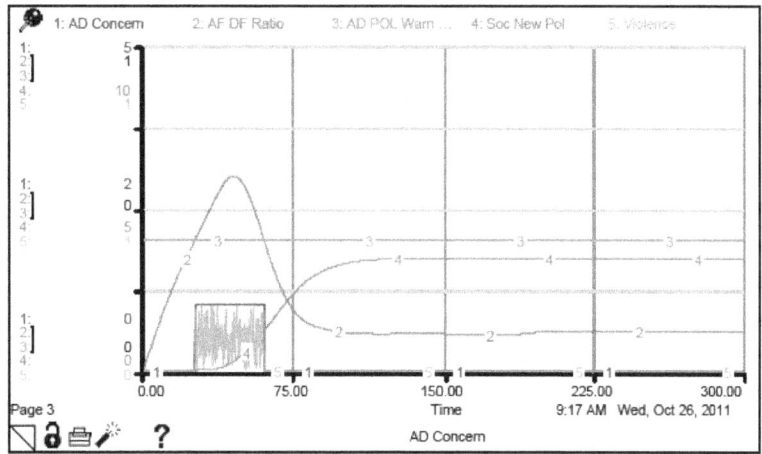

**Figure 18. Model-generated output shows the production of violent activity (*Violence*) and (*AD Concern*) output when the ratio of affected to disaffected individuals rises above the (*AD POL Warn*) threshold. The (*AD Concern*) output triggers policy cycle-based activities that generate instructions for creating a new policy (*Soc New Pol*).**

## POLICY CYCLE MODELS CAN REPRESENT THE MANAGEMENT OF SOCIETAL VIOLENCE LEVELS AND ENTITY SECURITY POLICIES[23]

Policy cycle models for the *Management of Societal Viol ence Levels and Entity Security* have been developed and im plemented in system s dynamics software (Appendix 6). A key new feature of these and the other polic y cycle models in this paper is the inclusion of properties that are assumed to reflect the im pact of corruption in underm ining the policy-related actions of a government entity. In the following studies, polic y cycle-related corrupti on reduced the im pact of policies aim ed at reducing violence and incr easing security. Corruption increased violence levels and prevented increased security-related processes from being implemented.

### A Social Policy Cycle Model for the Management of Violence

*A Social Policy Cycle Model for the Management of Violence* has been developed. Increasing rates of policy-related infor mation transfer in the absence of corruption can reduce the level of societal violence caused by disaffection. Figure 19 presents the key features of the model. Details of model implementation are described in Appendix 6, Figure A6.1. Input to the m odel represents policy concerns related to the levels of disaffection and violence. Those concerns trigger actions assumed to repr esent the formulation and implementation of social policy aim ed at reducing disaffection and vi olence. Those actions are fo llowed by actions assum ed to represent the evaluation and change of an ex isting policy involving eith er new policy creation and/or termination. Corruption is assumed to act by reducing the input to policy formulation and implementation and new policy generation acti ons. New policy actions would be aim ed at reducing violence levels by increasing satisfaction levels within a notional population.

---

[23] Details of the implementation of this model are presented in Appendix 6.

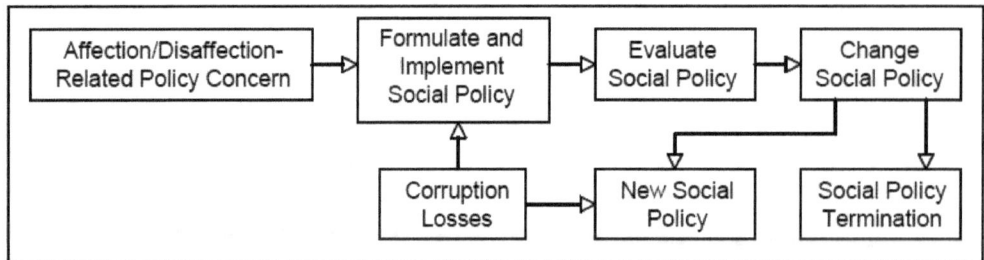

**Figure 19. Key features of the Social Policy Cycle Model with policy-related corruption.**

Selected results obtained from the use of the Social Policy Cycle model with different settings of the policy cycle parameters are shown in Fi gures 20, 21, 22, 23, and 24 (also Appendix 6). The (*Soc Pol Sensitiv*) parameter was set at 0.2 and the ( *Sec PolSens*) parameter was set at zero, thereby preventing contributions from Security Policy Cycle activities. Studies were undertaken in which the Policy Cycle param eters were set at 0.8 (an 80 percent transf er of information per time step) or 0.1 (10 percent per time step) and either with or without the influence of corruption.

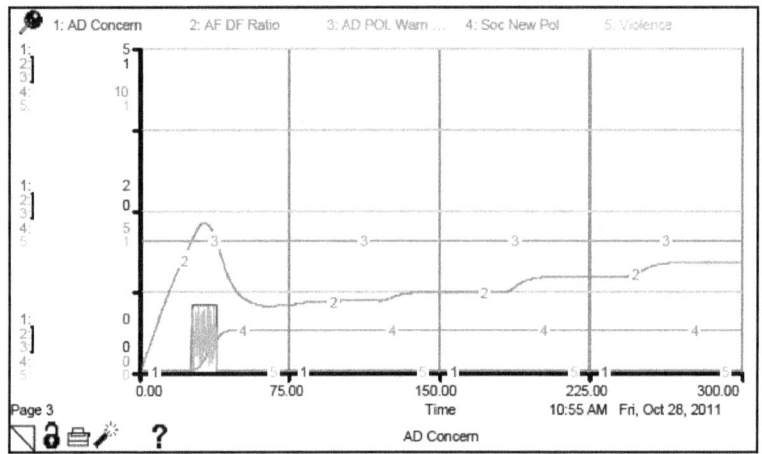

**Figure 20. Social Policy Cycle parameters set at 0.8 and corruption 0.0 generates a single burst of violent activity (*Violence*) when (*AF DF Ratio*) exceeds the (*AD POL Warn*) threshold.**

- Social Policy Cycle param eter values of 0.8 and corruption levels of 0.0 reduce violence levels (Figure 20): Cycle param eters social policy evaluation ( *Soc Eval Inpt*), social policy change ( *Soc Chnge Inpt*), social policy term ination (*Soc Term Inpt*), and new social policy (*Soc New Inpt*) set at 0.8 represent an 80-percent transfer rate per time step between entities. W ithout corruption, the corruption of new policy (*Soc CorrRte NewPol* ) and formulate and implem entation activities (*Soc F&I Corrupt*) were set at 0. These settings genera te a single short period of violent activity. That period stops when policy-base d actions reduce the le vel of disaffection below the warning threshold. In this case, relatively rapid m igration takes place through these entities: social policy for mulate and implement (*Soc F&I Tot*), social policy evaluation (*Soc Eval Tot* ), social po licy change (*Soc Chnge Tot I* ), social policy termination (*Soc Term*), and new social policy (*Soc New Pol* ). New polic y actions increase the lev el of satisfaction and re duce the le vel of disaffection in a relatively rapid m anner in the absence of corruption. Those inputs create a single

22

period of violence ( *Violence*), which is term inated as th e new policy leads to an increase in satisfaction and a corresponding reduction in disaffection (Figure 20).

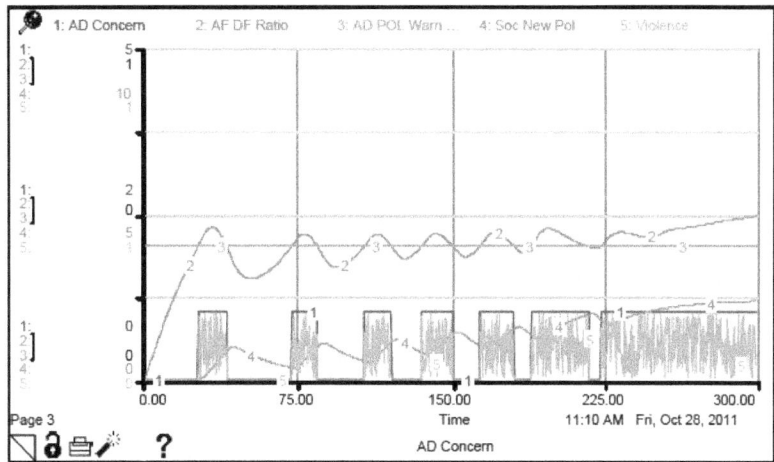

**Figure 21. Setting the Social Policy Cycle parameters at 0.8 and corruption parameters at 0.04 generated bursts of violent activity followed by continuous violence because of an inability caused by corruption of a government entity to reduce disaffection to sufficiently low levels where violence does not occur.**

- Social Policy Cycle parameter values of 0.8 and corruption levels of 0.04 can increase the duration of violence (Figure 21): Those inputs create conditions in which multiple bursts of violent activity are followed by a period of continued violence as government policies impacted by corruption are unable to reduce disaffection to sufficiently low levels in order to prevent violence. Corruption could be caused by use of trafficker-generated resources th at interfere with those governm ent-related actions aimed at inc reasing the le vel of satisfaction and decreasing the leve l of societal violence. Multiple bursts of violence reflect an inability to create a permanent reduction in the level of disaffection. Corruption could be funded by narcotics trafficker resources and lead to increased levels of violen ce. Violent events cou ld destabilize government entities an d lead to an increase in trafficker and terrorist influence within the society, for example.

- Social Policy Cycle parameter values of 0.1 and corruption levels of 0.0 can increase the duration of violence (Figure 22) and create conditions that produce a single period of violent activity of longer duration than that generated with policy cycle param eter values set at 0.8 (Figu re 20). Violence occurs when the level of disaffection exceeds threshold levels. Slower policy cycle-related actions reduce the rate of policy-related actions aimed at reducing disaffection. Policy cycle parameter values of 0.1 represent a transmission of 10 percent of notional in formation per time step, significantly less than the 80-percent rate mentioned above (Figures 20 and 21). The slow er rate might represent normal practice and the higher ra te an em ergency fast-track response to increased levels of societal violence, for example.

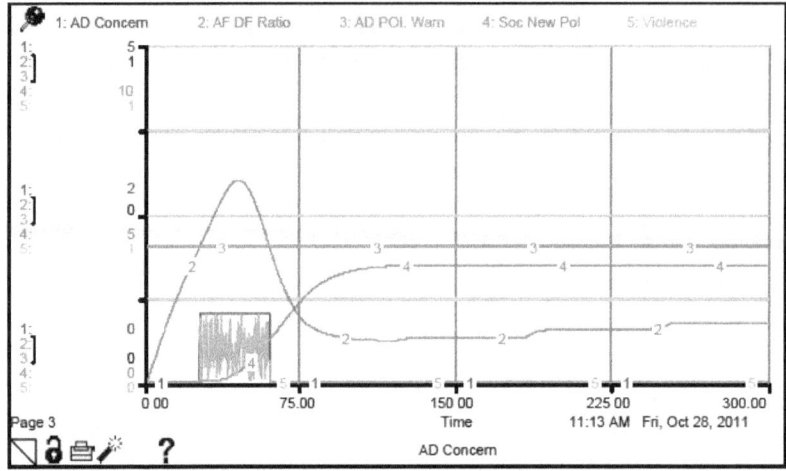

**Figure 22. Social Policy Cycle parameters set at 0.1 and corruption levels of 0.0 generate a longer period of violence compared with the situation involving parameter values of 0.8 (Figure 20) when the (*AF DF Ratio*) exceeds the (*AD POL Warn*) threshold.**

- Social Policy Cycle parameter values of 0.1 and corruption levels of 0.04 can increase the duration of violence (Figure 23). Slower notional information transmission rates coupled with corruption create con ditions that produce a s ingle period of violence followed by continuous violent ac tivity. Activities in the ( *Soc F&I Tot*), (*Soc Eval Tot*), (*Soc Chnge Tot*), (*Soc Term*), and (*Soc New Pol*) entities are s lower than with the Policy Cycle parameters set at 0.8. This represents the inability of the government entity to generate policies that are adequate to reduce disaffection-related violence.

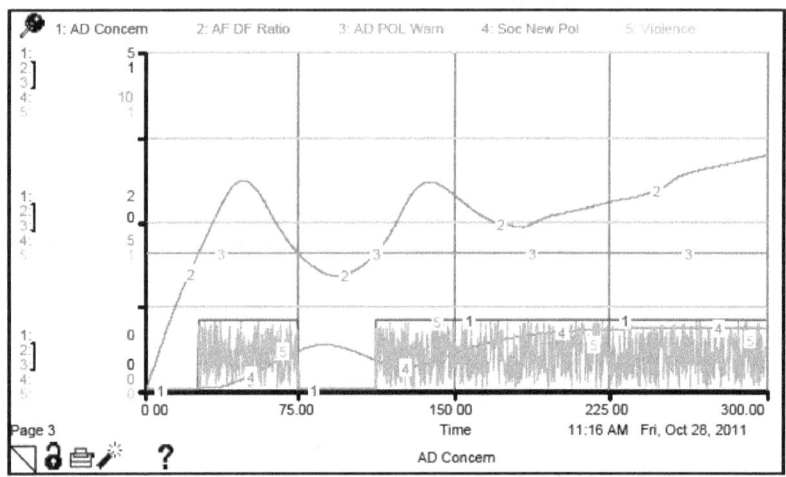

**Figure 23. Social Policy Cycle parameter values of 0.1 and corruption levels of 0.04 generated a period of violent activity followed by continuous violence. Compare Figure 23 with Figure 21, which reflects the impact of Social Policy Cycle parameters set at 0.8.**

These preliminary experiments have demonstrated that modeled policy cycle-related intervention can act to reduce the level of disaffection in a notional populat ion by increasing the level of satisfaction. Reduced levels of disaffection can reduce the level and duration of violence within a society. Corruption of the policy cycle process ca n reduce or even stop the disaffection-reducing actions, including implementation of new government policy cycle-generated policies. The level of societal violence is assumed to be determined by the ratio of disaffected to the total number of affected and disaffected individu als. Violence co uld occur when that ratio exceeds a value tha t reflects the historical behavior of a society of interest. Higher le vels of violence can be created by increasing the overall level of disaffection; lo wer violence levels can occur with relatively lower levels of disaffection caused by increased policy-based societal satisfaction.

Policy cycle-generated events that reduce the level of disaffection can act to redu ce overall violence levels. Even relatively m odest levels of corruptio n can cau se a reduction in policy effectiveness. It is as sumed that co rruption could be m ediated by th e infusion of trafficker-generated resources into the policym aking processes of a national governm ent or other policymaking entities. Higher levels of violence can act to reduce the legitimacy of a government so that trafficker-gen erated corruption can p rovide a b asis for facilitating terrorist actions. Increased terrorist effectiveness cou ld also faci litate trafficker actions by reducing the num ber and extent of government-led counter-narcotics actions.

## A Security Policy Cycle Model for Entity Security Management

A *Security Policy Cycle Model* for the m anagement of entity security has been developed and implemented in system s dynamics software. Figure 24 presents the key features of the m odel. Details of implem entation of the model are shown in Appendix 6, Figure A6.3. Input to the policy cycle model represents policy concerns rela ted to the impact of casualty levels generated by notional terrorist activities. Terrorist actions can occur when targets are vulnerable and trained terrorists are available. In the model, terrorist actions trigger policy cycle-based actions assumed to represent the formulation and implementation of a security policy. That policy is responsive to existing conditions and involves ev aluation and change of an exis ting policy, creation of a new policy, and/or term ination of the existing policy. Corruption is assumed to act by reducing the input to the policy formulation- and im plementation-related activities. Corruption could also reduce the input responsible for generating a new security-related policy, thereby increasing the likelihood that terrorist events might occur because of an inability to increase security policy.

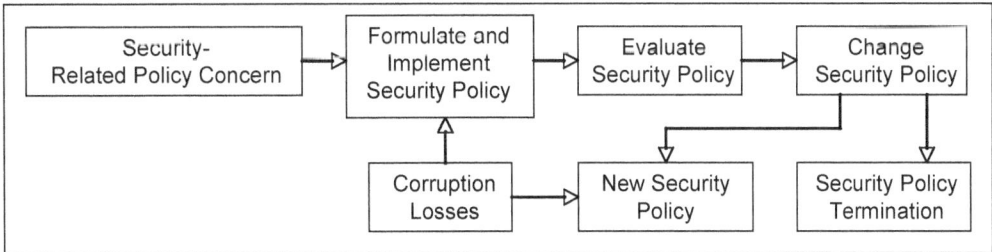

**Figure 24. Key features of the Security Policy Cycle Model with policy-related corruption.**

Activities within the implemented model are triggered when the number of actual terrorist events (*TotATActEvents*) is greater than zero (Appendix 6, Figure A6.3). The m agnitude of policy-related responses is also determined by the level of security-policy-related sensitivity (*Sec Pol Sensitiv*). Policy-related changes are intended to raise the thres hold above which terrorist actions would be triggered when the random ly generated number (which can vary between 0 and 100) exceeds the threshold. Under some circumstances, excessive policy cycle output levels cause the threshold to increase above 100, representing som e form of excess security level f or triggering

25

terrorist actions. Corruption-related activities, by contrast, can re duce the threshold and increase the likelihood that notional terro rist actions w ould be trigge red when the generated random number exceeds the threshold value.

Two studies were undertaken to exam ine the imp act of (1) increasing the speed of notional policy-related information transfer within the sec urity-related policy cyc le model by increasing the value of the policy cycle parameters in the absence of corruption, and (2) increasing the level of corruption within the policy cyc le model at f ixed information transfer rates. Those studies demonstrate that higher rates of notional inform ation transfer within the cy cle can gene rate instructions that cause a relatively rapid increase in the s ecurity threshold, thereby reducing the likelihood of terrorist actions fr om taking place. Higher corrupti on levels reduce the level of policy-related changes in security levels and c an lead to increas ed numbers of terroris t events and casualties. Results are presented in Figures 25 and 26.

| PCM parms | Fin Sec Lvl | Tot Evnts | Act Evnts | Sec New Pol | Tot Casult |
|-----------|-------------|-----------|-----------|-------------|------------|
| 0 | 88.7 | 70 | 27 | 0 | 1496 |
| 0.02 | 95.8 | 57 | 25 | 10.5 | 1358 |
| 0.04 | 102 | 39 | 21 | 16 | 1114 |
| 0.06 | 105 | 32 | 16 | 18 | 846 |
| 0.08 | 106.8 | 29 | 15 | 19 | 840 |
| 0.1 | 108 | 26 | 13 | 20 | 727 |

**Figure 25. Increased rate of policy-related information transfer can reduce total terrorist-generated casualties. Impact of policy cycle parameter values (*PCM parms*) on security level (*Fin Sec Lvl*), potential (*Tot Events*) and actual (*Act Evnts*) terrorist events, and total casualties (*Tot Casult*) with security political sensitivity (*Sec Pol Sens*) set at 0.2; security investment (*Sec Invest*) was set at 0.01; and corruption was set at zero.**

- The impact of policy cy cle information transfer rate on security levels and terrorist-related casualties: Increased rate of policy-related information transfer can reduce total terrorist-generated casualties (Figure 25). The first study investigated the impact of increasing the speed of notional information transfer within the security-related policy cycle model from 0 to 0.1 (10-percent transfer per time step) on the potential and actual num ber of terrorist events a nd the production of notional casualties. Increasing the rate of policy cycle-related information transfer reduces the num ber of events and the num ber of cas ualties. (1) Baseline conditions were established by setting the policy cycle param eters at ze ro and preventing policy cycle involvem ent and policy cycle-m ediated security investments. Notional security lo sses perhaps because of increased vulnera bility, of 0.0004 (0.04 percent) per time step caused the security threshold to dec line from 100 to a f inal security lev el (*Fin Sec Lvl*) of 88.7 during a no tional period of 300 days. Th e reduced secu rity threshold permitted generation of 70 possible terrorist events ( *Tot Evnts*) of which only 27 ( *Act Evnts*) actually took place because of the lack of trai ned terrorist personne l. Those events created some 1,496 notional casualties ( *Tot Casult*)). (2) Policy cycle parameters set at 0.1 provide an increased investm ent in security that can offset the im pact of security losses. Under these conditions, the security threshold initially decreased and then increased to 108, which is above th e initial value of 100, a nd represents conditions in which entities are not vulnera ble to terrorist attack. Model-generated data suggest that under policy-related security conditions of transient vulnerability, 13 of 26 actual terrorist events with 727 casualties occurred (Figure 25).

- The impact of corruption on security levels and total te      rrorist-related casualties: Increased levels of corruption can lead to      increased num bers of terrorist-generated casualties. (Figure 26).    The second security study in      vestigated the im pact of corruption on security level, num ber of terro rist events, and the level o f casualties. The policy cycle param eters were held at  0.1 and the corruption  parameters varied from 0 to 0.1. Studies show that with zer o corruption, the policy cycle process results in a final security level of 108, some 13 ac   tual terrorist events  that create 727 total casualties take place. In creasing the level of  corruption to 0. 1 prevents policy cycle-related increases in security  levels from  taking place. Th is creates a final secu rity level of 89.6, which results in 27 actual te    rrorist events with  1,496 total casualties taking place.

| Corrruption | Fin Sec Lvl | Tot Evnts | Act Evnts | Sec New Pol | Tot Casult |
|-------------|-------------|-----------|-----------|-------------|------------|
| 0 | 108 | 26 | 13 | 20 | 727 |
| 0.02 | 94.8 | 50 | 26 | 4 | 1396 |
| 0.04 | 91.7 | 64 | 27 | 1.8 | 1496 |
| 0.06 | 90.6 | 65 | 27 | 1 | 1496 |
| 0.08 | 90 | 66 | 27 | 0.7 | 1496 |
| 0.1 | 89.6 | 66 | 27 | 0.5 | 1496 |

**Figure 26. Increased levels of corruption can lead to increased numbers of terrorist-generated casualties. Impact of policy cycle corruption (*Corruption*) on security level (*Fin Sec Lvl*), potential (*Tot Events*) and actual (*Act Evnts*) events, and total casualties (*Tot Casult*) with security political sensitivity (*Sec Pol Sens*) set at 0.2, the security investment (*Sec Invest*) set at 0.01, and the policy cycle parameters set at 0.1.**

It could be assum ed that synergetic interactio ns involving narcotics tr afickers and terrorists could  involve use of traffick   er  resources to corrupt the      counter-narcotics  policymaking processes.  Such actions could block attem   pts  to  increase  security an d  lead to an increased number and scope of terrorist events with highe r casualty levels. This could create an increas ed perception of a government that wa s unable to protect the citizenry  and lead to increased levels of disaffection and create further violence. T hose changes could act to underm ine a government and facilitate future trafficker and terrorist actions, to the benefit of both traffickers and terrorists.

Higher security thresholds can have the effect of preventing terrorist events from taking place as the result of a notiona l increase in security or  reduction in  entity vu lnerability. Such changes could reflect an increase in the  alert status and responsiveness of  entities involved in setting and implementing  security policy. Increased respo    nsiveness  can reduce vulnerabilities and the number of terrorist events and associated casualties that could occur. S tudies have examined the impact of c orruption on the abi lity of policy-related chang es in alert s tatus and res ponsiveness and  the production of notional casualties. C     orruption  can prevent policy-related security increases from taking place, th ereby increasing vulnerability and fostering the perception of an inability of a government to protect its people.

# SUMMARY, DISCUSSION, AND A WAY FORWARD

This paper has provided a review of the drug tra fficking and terrorist domains as well as m eans to counter their activ ities. This was accom plished through the develop ment of models for dru g trafficking, terrorist activities, and the role of the policymaker in countering their activities. More specifically, the conclusions of the overall study are as follows:

- The study included an investiga tion of the counter-narcotics activities and the role of efforts aimed at converting tr affickers into double agents. <u>Model-generated data closely resembled actual reports of tons of disrupted narco tics substances detected in 2008, 2009, and 2010.</u> A policy cycle m odel was deve loped and used to study the potential impact of increased levels of policymaking support as well as corruption of the policy process on the ability to form double agents and to disrupt trafficker activities. <u>Increased rates of policy cycle activity increased the am ount of narcotics disruption. However, increased levels of corruption reduced those levels.</u>

- <u>Model-generated results show that p olicymaking can le ad to a reduction in the leve l of deprivation, disaffection, and violence and that policy-related effects can be inhibited by corruption, which can change th e overall political dynam ics of societies of interest.</u> The policies m ay range from providing social services, em ployment, medical and housing assistance, and so fort h. This is sim ilar to what Hezbollah provides to poor communities in Lebanon and other Diaspora locations. The goal is to win the hearts and m inds of the people. The prevention of actions taken by the government tend to increase the duration of disaffection-related violence, and the y also increase the num ber of dis affected individuals available for recruitment into terrorist training programs. In order to accurately assess this impact, it is necessary to have data that provide the range of possi ble actions taken by terrorist organizations and their impact on the population. A leadi ng counter-terrorism expert conducted an extensive interview process of prisoners in I srael that r eveals the rationale f or undertaking terrorist acts such as planti ng improvised explosive devices (IED) in public places. The level of disaffection range s from ideological concerns to personal grievances and family tragedies as a result of the occupation.

- Modeling the combined terrorist-narcotics tr afficker threat to national security has involved production of several component models, including the following:
  - *A Societal Deprivation, Disaffection, Recruitment, Advanced Terror ist Training, and Narco-Terrorist Support Model* that illustrates how notional individuals deprived of key res ources can become disaffected and recruited and trained to become advanced terrorists.
  - *An Entity Security and Terroris t Activity Model* that illustrates the a ttack of notional targets by teams of trained terrorists.
  - *Entity Security and Vio lence Generation Models* describe how deprived and disaffected individuals m ay become violent and how such violence can increase the level of perceived deprivation and disaffection.
  - *Social and Security Policy Cycle Models* that represent the processes of identifying a problem and form ulating, implementing, evaluating, changing, and/or term inating a policy in response to perceived need, as

well as the im pact of corruption in preventing successful policy-related outcomes.

- <u>Model-based studies also show that the av ailability of trained terrorists needed f or operations is a rate-lim iting factor and that vulnerable targets of opportunity m ay not be attacked because trained te rrorist operatives are lacking.</u> This sugg ests that the narcotics trafficker networks could perf orm important intelligence functions by identifying vulnerable targets and alerting terrorist organizations to pre-pos ition operatives in order to take advantage of oppor tunities. Trafficker networks could also increase target vulnerability by creating climates of fear and reduced social activity in target areas. These potential actions by the car tel networks could be of great value to the terrorists and m ay be worth the financ ial investment they would m ake in such cartel organizations. In order to ass ess the value, a detailed examination of specifi c indictments and the con tribution of intelligence are r equired. However, most of the unsealed cases focus on the tactics used by the cartels in m oving shipments of narcotics and the actions of facilitators in th is process. A distinct connectivity between criminal and terrorist groups is well known. Their interaction is based on the ability of each group to provi de a critical service to a nother and profiting from the transaction. The accomplishm ent here is beyond the academ ic exercise of m odel development but is focused on the interaction and the benefits/gains that are achieved.

Looking forward, additional m odel-based studies ar e needed to assess the effect of narcotics trafficker and terrorist involvement in at least the following activities:

- Support to terrorist training capacity and the increased rate of recruitm ent of disaffected individuals as terrorists

- The supply of trained terrorist personnel, re sources, and facilities to support advanced terrorist training and operational activities

- The effect of narcotics trafficker and te rrorist involvement in and the im pact of corruption on security-related protective policy-based measures

- The effect of corruption on implem entation of governm ent policies aim ed at preventing social deprivation, disaffection, and violence

- The effect of terrorist and narcotics trafficker personnel deploym ent on entity vulnerability and intelligence collection actions.

The authors believe that m odeling these activit ies can provide a deeper understanding of the relationship between drug traffi cking and terror ist activities as w ell as the role of the policymaker in countering these threats. Additi onal insight can be generated by studies that identify values for the assum ed model param eters, potentially leading to the development of enhanced and more realistic models. Those models could support production of new facilities for counter-terrorist and counter-narcotics policymaking and decisionmaking.

# APPENDICIES 1 TO 6: IMPLEMENTATION OF THE MODELS IN SYSTEMS DYNAMICS SOFTWARE

Details of the m odels developed and used in th e studies reported in th is paper are presented below.

## APPENDIX 1: A NARCOTICS, COUNTER-NARCOTICS, AND TRAFFICKER DOUBLE AGENT MODEL

### Preliminary Model-Building Considerations

The models described in this paper were developed and im plemented in STELLA™, a commercially available systems dynamics-based software system (http://www.iseesystems. com) by Woodcock. Figure A1.1 and other figures are screenshots take n from the models developed and used as described in this paper. Pr ogramming in STELLA™ involves dragging icons representing different properties and capabilities onto a workspace p rovided by the system and forming functional links between appropriate entities. Key com ponents include, but are not limited to, stocks, flows, converters, and actio n converters. Figure A1.1 represents a sam ple model of the Flow *Input* to a *Process* entity (represented by the rectan gular stock construct) at a rate determined by the *Input Rate* parameter. Output from the *Process* entity to a *Product* entity takes place at a rate determined by multiplica tion of the v alue of the *Process* and *Output Rate* parameters. Once the model is assembled, the system asks the user for information and data.

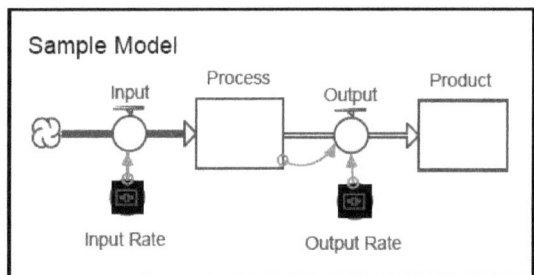

**Figure A1.1. The Sample Model structure involves stocks, flows, converters, and action converters provided by the STELLA™ system.**

```
Process(t) = Process(t - dt) + (Input - Output) * dt
INIT Process = 0

INFLOWS:
Input = Input_Rate
OUTFLOWS:
Output = Output_Rate*Process
Product(t) = Product(t - dt) + (Output) * dt
INIT Product = 0

INFLOWS:
Output = Output_Rate*Process
Input_Rate = 0.1
Output_Rate = 0.05
```

**Figure A1.2. Sample Model source code is generated automatically by STELLA™.**

30

User development of the m odel structure, m odel relationships, and param eter values (Figure A1.1) sets the scene for autom atic source code generation for the model (Figure A1.2). The rectangular icons inside the *Input* and *Output Rate* converter icons (Figur e A1.1) represent the fact that sliders have been implemented to permit user selection of specif ic *Process* and *Output Rate* parameter values. Those sliders are shown in the model control panel in Figure A1.3. Sliders permit rapid user selection of paramete r values during experim ental studies with th e model. The control panel can be constructed to provide num erical data displays and other information. In this case *Input* and *Output Rates* set at 0.1 generate *Process* and *Product* values of 1 and 9, respectively. STELLA™ also prov ides a graphical display facility that has been used to display the incre ase with tim e of the *Process* and *Product* parameters (Figure A1.4). The system permits user selection of Run Specificati ons that define the duration and other properties of the runtime of the model. In this case the runtime has been set at a notional 100 days.

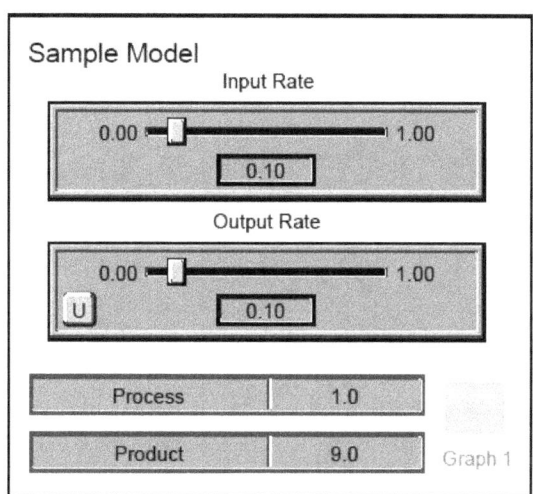

**Figure A1.3. Sample Model control panel showing sliders and numerical data displays.**

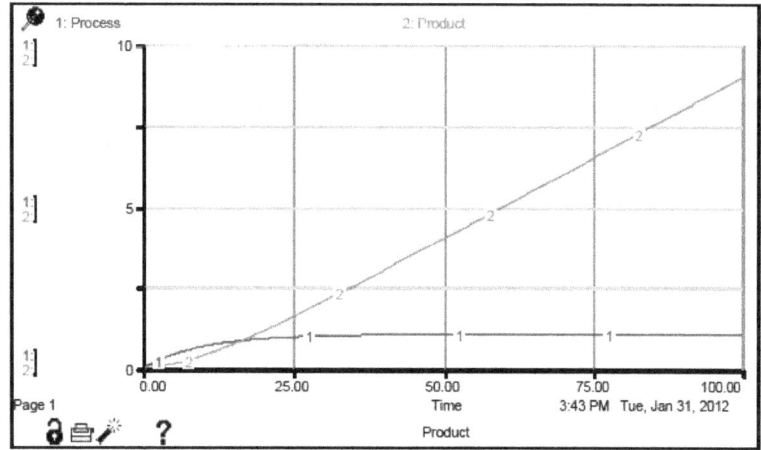

**Figure A1.4. Sample Model graphical output showing calculated *Process* and *Product* values for a notional 100 days.**

It is hoped that this brief introduction to the use of STELLA™ ha s provided an adequate foundation to perm it the reader to access th e following descriptions of the d evelopment, implementation, and use of the m odels described below. Additional information can be obtained from the http://www.iseesystems.com website.

## Implementation of the Narcotics, Counter-narcotics, and Trafficker Double Agent Model

Implementation of the *Narcotics, Counter-narcotics, and Trafficker Double Agent* model in STELLA™ (http://www.iseesysystems.com) is shown in Figure A1.5. The m odel provides a notional representation of the process of converti ng traffickers into double agents and using the information they m ight provide to disrupt additional shipments of narcotics. Details of these activities are presented below.

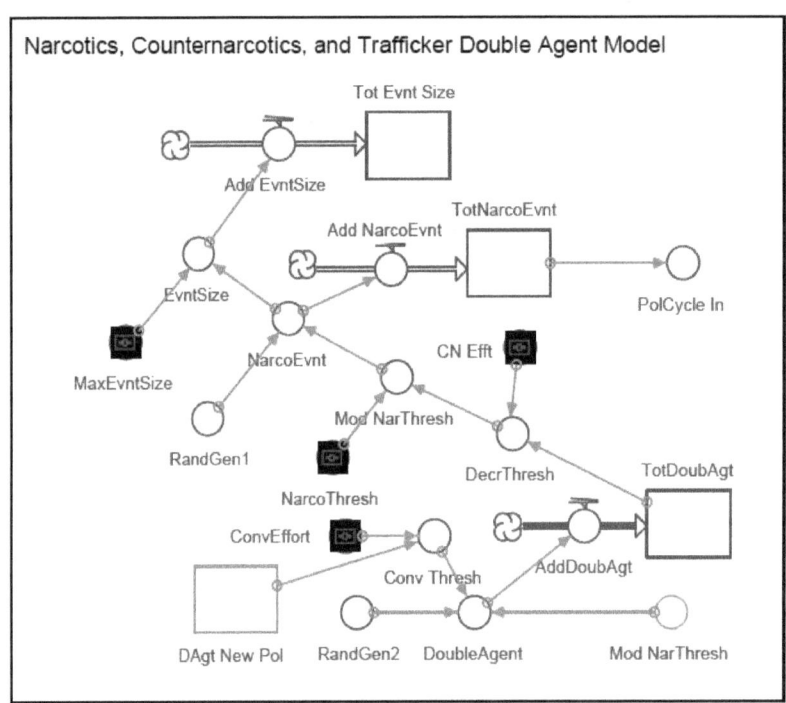

**Figure A1.5. Counter-narcotics model that represents the impact of creating trafficker double agents on the number and size of narcotics seizure activities. The model also provides output to (*PolCycle In*) and input from a policy cycle-based management model (*DAgt New Pol*) described in the text.**

Narcotics substance seizures or disruptions are assum ed to take place when a random ly generated number (*RandGen1*) is g reater than a user-s elected threshold value ( *NarcoThresh*) (Figure A1.5). The threshold for detection or disr uption of narcotics substa nces can be modified by the effect of the gene ration of double agents, ( *Mod Nar Thresh* ) as described below. Disruption events are represented b y the (*NarcoEvnt*) parameter which has v alue 1 for a m odel-generated event and 0 otherwise. Non-zero (*NarcoEvnt*) data trigger anot her random number generator (*EvntSize*), the output of which ranges from 0 to the user-selected ( *MaxEvntSize*) parameter representing the m aximum size of disrupt ed narcotics shipments. The total event size (*Tot Evnt Size*) is formed from the addition of all even ts; the total number of counter-narcotics events is represented in the model as the (*TotNarcoEvnt*) parameter. Model facilities were also created that provide input to a policy cycle m anagement model (*PolCycle In*), and output from the policy cycle m odel can change the policy on double agent recruitment ( *DAgt NewPol*). The policy cycle model is described below (Appendix 2). Use of that model enabled consideration of the impact of the rate at which polic ymaking could take place and how policym aking might be influenced by corruption. Data on th e total number of narcotics seizures and the to tal size of those seizures was collected and displayed both numerically and graphically.

The conversion of narcotics traffi ckers into double agen ts is represented by a process in which conversion is assum ed to take place when a random number generated by a random number generator (*RandGen2*) is greater than a use r-selected threshold determined by the value of the user-selected *ConvEffort* and *Conv Thresh* parameters (Figure A1.5). Higher thresholds represent conditions where such conversion is relatively unlikely to take place. Increased conversion efforts are assum ed to reflect a lowering of the thresh old (*Mod Nar Thresh* ) representing conditions where a greater likelihood exists for the generated random number (*RandGen1*) to exceed the threshold and represent disruption of narcotics shipments.

The trafficker double agents ( *TotDoubAgt*) generated by the conversi on process are assum ed to provide information that could be used to de crease the threshold for detection of narcotics trafficker activities (*DecrThresh*). Actual narcotics detection was assumed to depend on the level of effort involved in converting trafficker -provided intelligence into operation al counter-narcotics activities represented by the (*CN Efft*) parameter. Higher levels of such efficiency are assumed to generate a greater likelihood for narc otics detection, seizure, or other types of disruption.

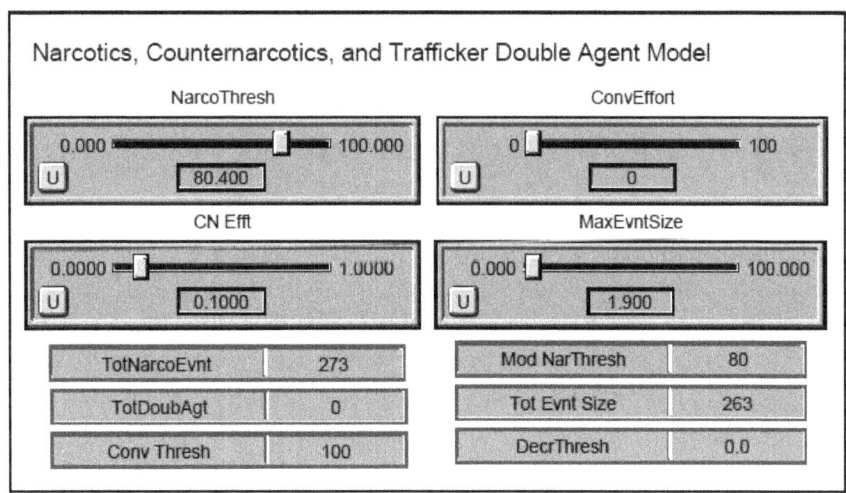

**Figure A1.6. Control panel for the Narcotics, Counter-narcotics, and Trafficker Double Agent Model permits the display of selected model outputs.**

The control panel for the Narcotics, Counter-nar cotics, and Trafficker Double Agent Model is shown in Figure A1.6. The panel perm its user se lection of the narcotics detection threshold (*NarcoThresh*; set at 80.4), counter-nar cotics effectiveness ( *CN Efft*; 0.1), double agent conversion effort (*ConvEffort*; 0), and maximum size of disturbed shipm ents (*MaxEvntSize*; 1.9) and their use in model-based studies, for example.

# APPENDIX 2: POLICY CYCLE MODELS CAN MANAGE TRAFFICKER DOUBLE AGENT CONVERSION POLICIES

A policy cycle model of policy aimed at increasing the level of effort to convert traffickers into double agents has been developed and implemented in systems dynamics software (Figure A2.1) The model has facilities that detect actions aimed at producing double agents. Notional policies are developed to enhance the rate of creation of those agents. A key feature of this model is the inclusion of properties that reflect the notional impact of corruption in undermining the counter-narcotics policy-related actions of a govern ment. Corruption inhibits the double agent recruitment process and reduces the am ount of na rcotics substances disr upted or disturbed by counter-narcotics actions.

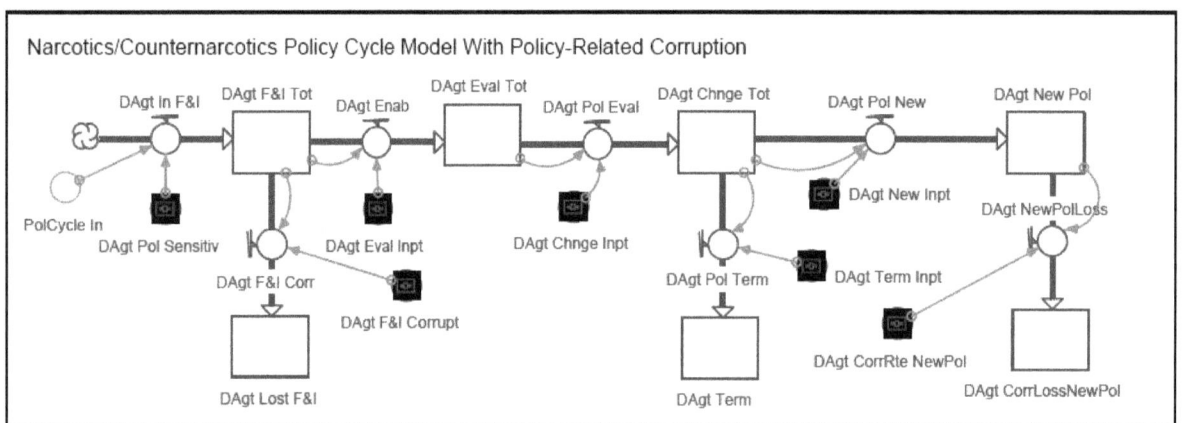

**Figure A2.1. Policy Cycle Model describing the creation of double agent generating policies. Policies supporting the creation of double agents can result in an increase the amount of narcotics substances disturbed by counter-narcotics actions; corruption of the policymaking process can reduce that amount. Double agent new policy (*DAgt New Pol*) provides input to the Narcotics, Counter-narcotics, and Trafficker Double Agent Model.**

Activities within the im plemented policy cycle m odel are trigg ered when the *TotNarcoEvnt* parameter is equal to 1 and the (*PolCycle In*) parameter is then set to 1 (Figures A1.5 and A2.1). Policy-related responses are also determ ined by the level of sensitivit y to double agent-related actions (*DAgt Pol Sensitiv*). Double agent policy cycle-relate d activities invol ve double agent policy formulation and im plementation (*DAgt F&I Tot*), double agent policy evaluation ( *DAgt Eval Tot*), double agent policy change ( *DAgt Change Tot*), new double agent policy creation (*DAgt New Pol*), and double agent policy term ination (*DAgt Pol Term*). These a ctivities take place at u ser-selected rates: policy evaluation ( *DAgt Eval Inpt*), policy change ( *DAgt Chnge Inpt*), new policy ( *DAgt New Inpt*), and policy term ination (*DAgt Term Inpt*), respectively. Corruption of the double agent poli cy formulation and implementation processes takes place at a rate determined by the (*DAgt F&I Corrupt*) parameter and corrupti on of the new double agent policy takes place at a rate determined by the (*DAgt CorrRte NewPol*)parameter. Output from the counter-narcotics model (Figure A1.5) (*PolCycle In*) triggers events in the policy cycle aimed at increasing the number of converted trafficker d ouble agents. The ability to increase the num ber of conversions can be af fected by corruption of the policym aking processes since that reduces the value of the (*DAgt New Pol*)parameter as well as the efforts involved in agent recruitm    ent (Figure A1.5).

The  control panel for the Double Agent Polic    y Cycle Model is shown in Figure A2.2. The control panel permits user selection of the following parameters: double agent policy sensitivity (*DAgt  Pol Sensitiv*; set at 0.0) ,  input  rate to double agent policy evaluation (   *DAgt  Eval Input*; 0.1), input rate to double agent policy change (*DAgt  Chnge Input*; 0.1), input rate to double agent policy termination (*DAgt  Term Input*; 0.1), input rate to   new  double agent policy ( *DAgt  New Input*; 0.1), new double agent po licy corruption rate ( *DAgt  CorrRte NewPol*; 0), and corruption of double agent policy formulation and implementation (*DAgt F&I Corrupt*; 0).

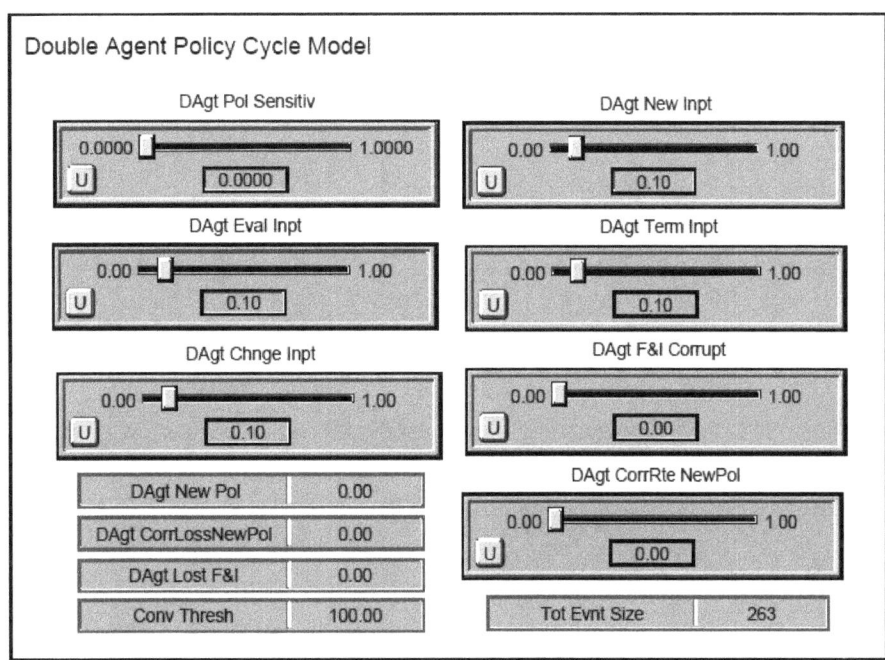

**Figure A2.2. Control panel for the Double Agent Policy Cycle Model shows slider value inputs and numerical output values of selected parameters.**

# APPENDIX 3: PROTOTYPE SOCIETAL DEPRIVATION, AFFECTION, DISAFFECTION, ADVANCED TERRORIST RECRUITMENT, TRAINING, AND NARCO-TERRORIST SUPPORT MODEL

Implementation of the Societal Deprivation, Affection, Disaffection, Advanced Terrorist Recruitment, Training, and Narco-Terrorist Su pport Model is shown in Figure A 3.1. In the model, affected individuals (*Affect*) are transformed into disaffected (*Disaffected*) individuals at rates determined by the level of deprivation (*DepLvl* and *Dep Enh*). Disaffected individuals can become affected by actions aim ed at increas ing the level of satisfaction either by existin g government policies (*SatLvl*) or by new governm ent policies (d etermined by the values of the (*Soc New Pol*) and p olicy multiplier (*PolMult*) entities). Both affected and disaffected individuals may be lost as casua lties as a re sult of terrorist actions (represented by the m odel-generated *Damage* parameter) and reduce the overall size of the populations of interest.

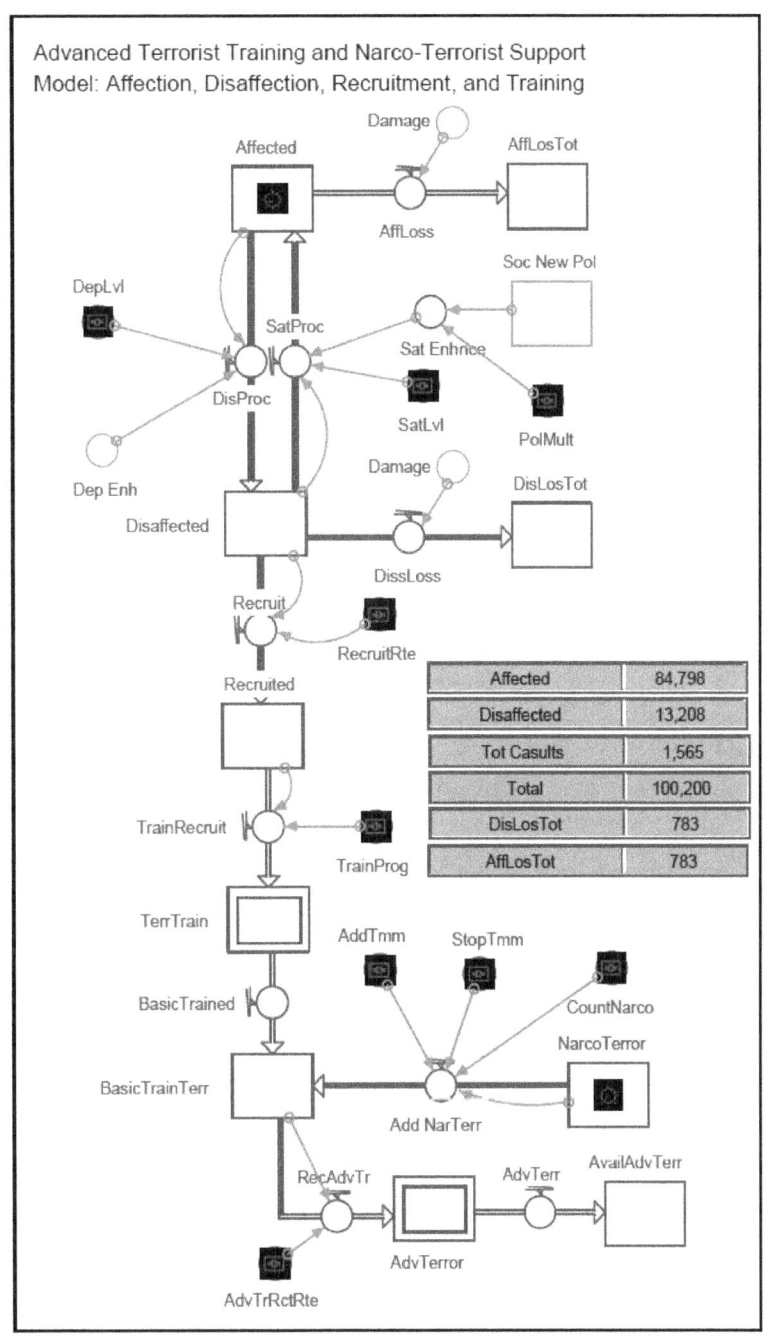

**Figure A3.1. Advanced Terrorist Recruitment, Training, and Narco-Terrorist Support Model represents the processes of affection, disaffection, recruitment, and production of basically trained and advanced terrorists. Those activities can be supported by the use of trafficker personnel and training facilities that create additional terrorists.**

Terrorists can be recruited from among disaffected individuals at a rate determined by the *RecruitRte* parameter. Recruited terrorists can undergo notional basic training (*TerrTrain*) and be recruited into advanced training (*AdvTerror*) at a rate determined by the (*AdvTrRctRte*) parameter generating available advanced terrorists (*AvailAdvTerr*). Training can be stopped by setting the (*TrainProg*) parameter to zero. Addition al individuals can be supplied by drug trafficker organizations (*NarcoTerror*) between tim es (*AddTmm*) and (*StopTmm*). The level of notional government actions against th at process is represented by the (*CountNarco*) process. In addition, narcotics trafficker re sources could be used to in crease the overall model-based capacities and throughput rates of the notional basic and advanced terrorist training facilities.

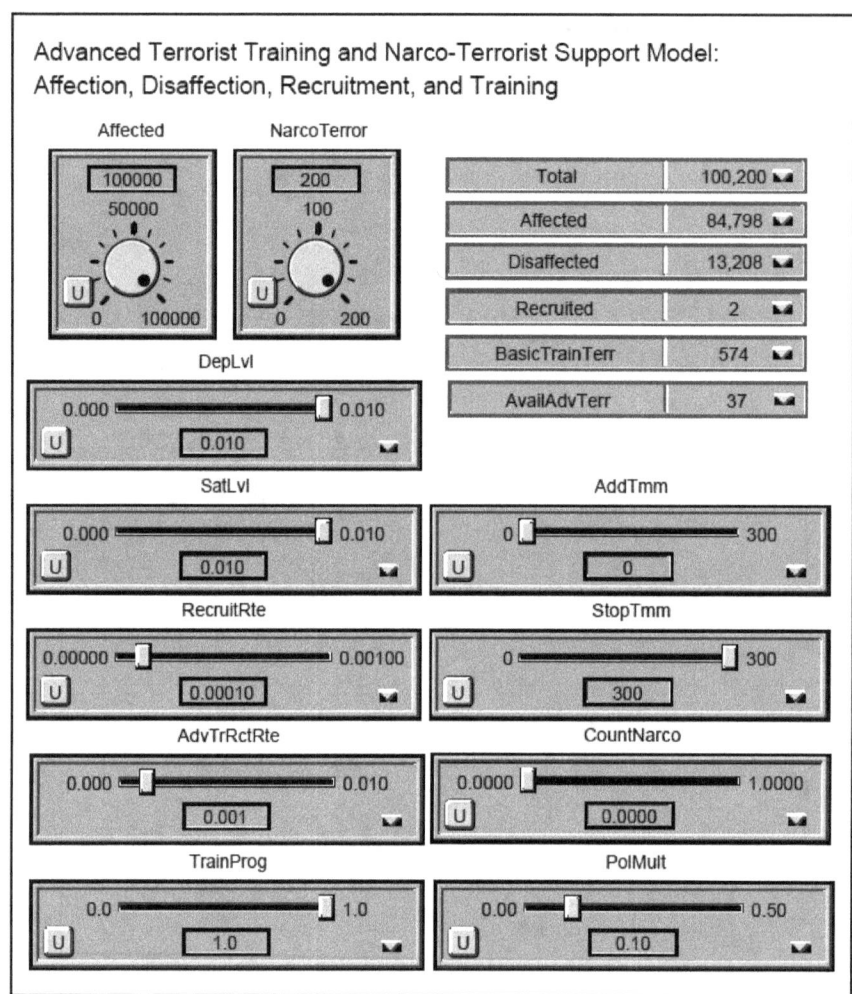

**Figure A3.2. The Advanced Terrorist Recruitment, Training, and Narco-Terrorist Support Model control panel provides capabilities for selecting model parameters and undertaking parameter impact analysis and assessment studies.**

The control panel for the Advanc ed Terrorist Training and Narc o-Terrorist Support Model is presented in Figure A3.2. User selection of m odel parameter values w ith the use of software sliders can provide an environm ent for undertaking studies of the im pact of m odel parameter values on model-generated outcomes. User-selected parameter values can include the following: initial affected population (*Affected*; set at 100,000); terrorists s upplied by narcotics traffickers (*Narcoterror*; 200); deprivation rate (*DepLvl*; 0.01); satisfaction rate (*SatLvl*; 0.01); recruitment rate for disaffected individuals ( *RecruitRte*; 0.0001); advanced terrori st recruiting rate (*AdvTrRctRte*; 0.001); training program in place ( *TrainProg*; 1); start tim e for adding trafficker personnel (*AddTmm*; 0); end time (*StopTmm*; 300); counter-narcotics effort (*CountNarco*; 0); and political multiplier (*PolMult*; 0.1).

Figure A3.3 provides a num erical cross-check to determine the involvement of all participants. Thus the total number of notional participants (*Total*) = 100,200 = ( *Affected*) + (*Disaffected*) + (*Recruited*) + (*AffLosTot*) + (*DisLosTot*) + (*TerrTrain*) + (*AvailAdvTerr*) + (*BasicTrainTerr*) + (*AdvTerror*) + (*NarcoTerror*).

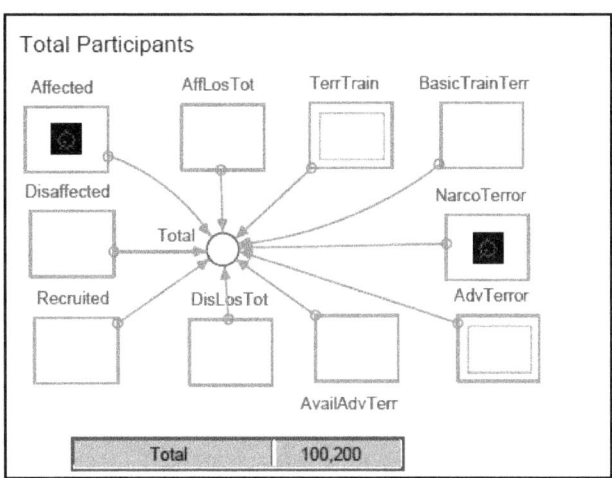

**Figure A3.3. Numerical cross-check to verify involvement of all notional participants in Figure A3.1.**

# APPENDIX 4: ENTITY SECURITY AND TERRORIST ACTIVITY MODELS

Implementation of the Entity Secu rity and Te rrorist Activity Models in system s dynamics software is shown in Figure A4.1. The key feature of the model is the representation of the level of entity security. The initial level of security (*SecLevel*), which can range from 100 ( most secure) to 0 (least secure), can be s elected by the user at the outset with the aid of the contro l panel (Figure A4.2). The security level (*SecLevel*) is increased by investment (*SecInvestRte*) and policy cycle-generated actions ( *Sec New Pol*). The level of security can be reduced by losses caused by lack of m aintenance and atte ntion and by hostile te rrorist actions (*SecLosRte*), for example.

Actual terrorist events (*ActAdvTerr*) can tak e place when adequate num bers of advanced terrorists (determined by the terrorist team size [*AdvTerTeamSize*] and num bers of advanced terrorists [*AvailAdvTerr*]) are available and security levels are appropriately low. Terrorist numbers are reduced by operatio nally generated casualties ( *Losses*). Terrorist losses are calculated based on the size of th e team and num ber of terrorist events, assuming that to tal terrorist casualties occur during each event.

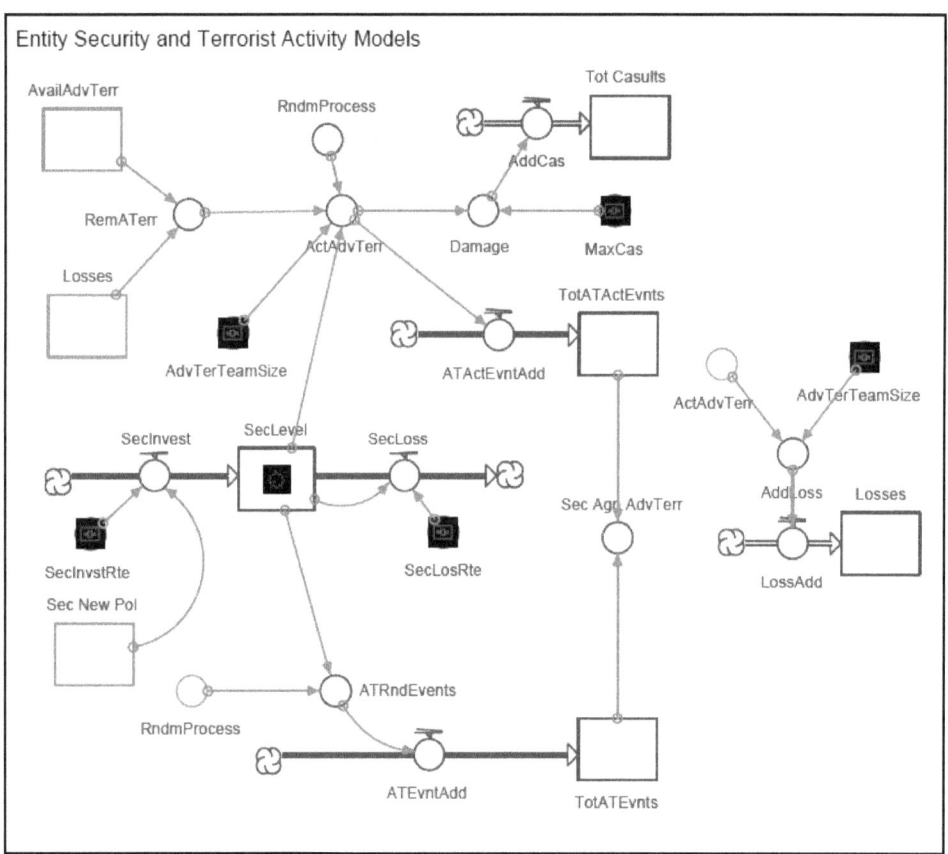

**Figure A4.1. Implementation of the Entity Security and Terrorist Activity Models provides a basis for undertaking studies of the impact of the number of trained terrorists and the vulnerability of targets on casualty levels. The key feature of the model is the level of security (*SecLevel*) that can be increased by investment in security and decreased by lack of maintenance and/or hostile actions.**

Potential events represent situations when the model-generated security level is be low the value of the model-generated random number (*RandomProcess*) but insufficient trained terrorists are available to take action. The ratio ( *Sec Agn AdvTerr*) of total actual (*TotATActEvents*) and total potential (*TotATEvents*) number of terrorist events provi des an indication of the relative availability of trained terrorists for operational purposes.

The Control Panel f or the Entity S ecurity and T errorist Activity Mode ls is pre sented in Figure A4.2. The Panel perm its user selection of the investm ent rate in m aintaining security (*SecInvstRte*; set at 0), the rate of loss of security ( *SecLosRte*; 0.0004), the maximum number of casualties per incident (*MaxCas*; 100), the terro rist group size (*AdvTerTeamSize*; 1), and initial security level (*SecLevl*; 100) of the of the modeled security environment.

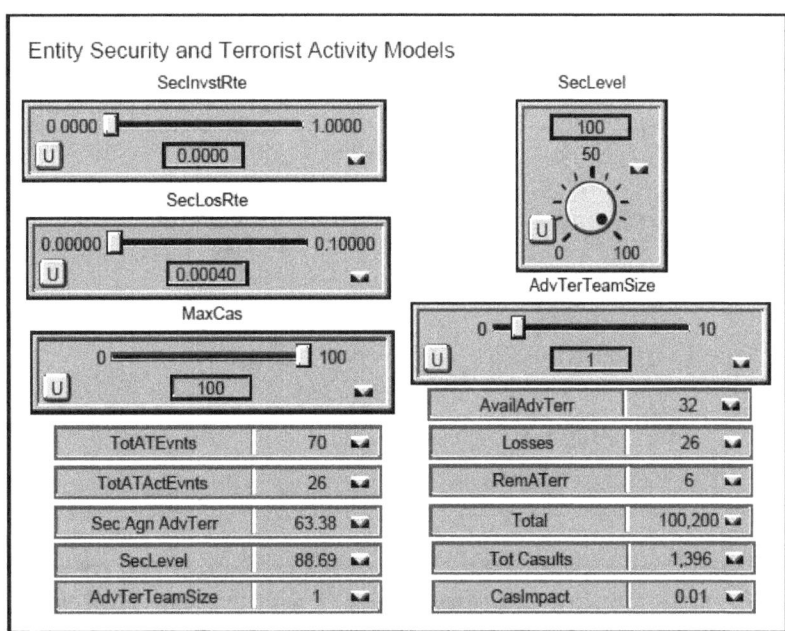

**Figure A4.2. The Control Panel for the Entity Security and Terrorist Activity Models shows selected parameter inputs and model-generated output. Settings indicate a maximum initial security level of 100, a security investment rate (*SecInvsRte*) of 0.0 and loss rate (*SecLosRte*) of 0.0004 (0 percent and 0.04 percent per time step, respectively), a maximum of 100 casualties (*MaxCas*) per incident and terrorist team size (*AdvTerTeamSize*) of 1. This creates 1,396 notional casualties (*Tot Casults*) in 26 incidents (*TotActEvnts*) that cause the loss of 26 terrorists (*Losses*).**

# APPENDIX 5: A VIOLENCE GENERATION MODEL

Implementation of the Violence G eneration Model in systems dynamics software is shown in Figure A5.1. The model calculates the level of violence (*Violence*) per incident and total violence (*Total Viol*) assumed to correspond to the ratio (*Disaffected/(Affected + Disaffected)*) of affected (*Affected*) and disaffected (*Disaffected*) individuals (*AF DF Ratio*), the affection-disaffection Political Warning threshold (*AD POL Warn Thresh*), and violence sensitivity (*Viol Sens*). The model also generates en hanced deprivation (*Dep Enh*) levels based on the values of a violence multiplier (*Viol Mult*), the level of violence (*Tot Viol*), and tota l casualties (*Tot Casults*) caused by terrorist events calculated by the Entity Security and Terrorist Activity Models (Appendix 4).

The control panel for the Violence Generation Model is shown in Figure A5.2. The Control panel permits user selection of the violence sensitivity (*Viol Sens*; set at 0.1) and multiplier (*Viol Mult*; 0.0008) and the (*AD POL Warn Thresh*; 0.2) parameters.

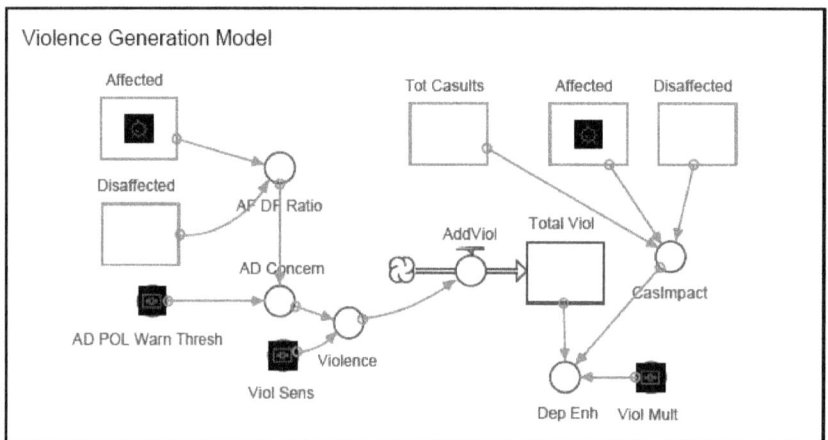

**Figure A5.1. Implementation of the Violence Generation Model. The model calculates the level of violence assumed to correspond to the ratio of (*Disaffected/(Affected + Disaffected)*) of disaffected and total affected and disaffected individuals and violence sensitivity as described in the text. The model also generates enhanced deprivation (*Dep Enh*) based on the level of violence and total casualties caused by terrorist events.**

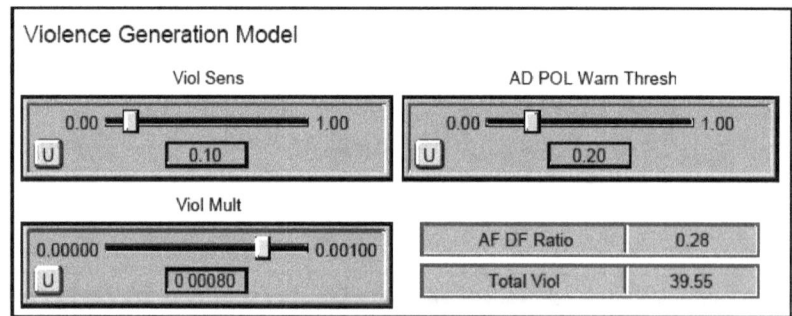

**Figure A5.2. The Violence Generation Model control panel permits user selection of the violence sensitivity (*Viol Sens*; set at 0.1), violence multiplier (*Viol Mult*; 0.0008), and the (*AD POL Warn Thresh*; 0.2) parameters.**

# APPENDIX 6: POLICY CYCLE MODELS CAN REPRESENT THE MANAGEMENT OF SOCIAL VIOLENCE AND ENTITY SECURITY POLICIES

A Social Policy Cycle Model for the m anagement of societa l violence levels and a Security Policy Cycle Model for the m anagement of entity security have been developed. Those m odels have been implem ented in system s dynamics software and used in a series of prelim inary studies. Details of the software implementation are presented below. Results of the studies are presented above.

## A Social Policy Cycle Model

*A Social Policy Cycle Model* for the management of societal violence has been developed. Figure A6.1 presents implementation of the m odel in systems dynamics software. Input to the m odel represents policy concerns related to the impact of levels of affection and disaffection and related levels of violence. Those concerns trigger noti onal actions assumed to represent the form ulation and implementation of social pol icy responsive to existing m odel-related conditions. These actions are followed by actions assumed to represent the evaluation and change of existing policy involving either the creation of a new policy and/or termination of an existing policy. Corruption is assumed to act by reducin g the input to policy form ulation and im plementation-related activities and to reduce the input responsible for generating a new policy aimed at increasing the overall level of satisfaction within the notional population.

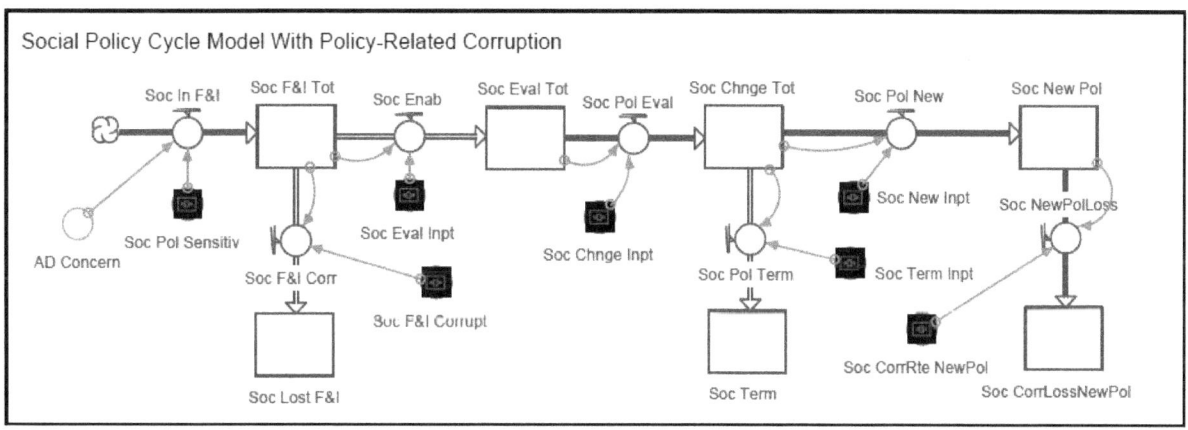

**Figure A6.1. Implementation of the Social Policy Cycle Model provides an environment for assessing the impact of Policy-Related Corruption on the production of new policies.**

Activities within the implemented model are tr iggered when the ratio of disaffected individuals compared with the to tal of affect ed and disaffected indiv iduals (*AD Concern*) exceeds a user-selected threshold (*AD POL Warn*) (Figure A6.1). Policy-related responses are also determ ined by the level of social-policy-related sensitivity (*Soc Pol Sensitiv*). Activities involve social policy formulation and implementation (*Soc F&I Tot*), evaluation (*Soc Eval Tot*), change (*Soc Change Tot*), new policy creation ( *Soc New Pol*), and policy term ination (*Soc Term*). These activ ities take place at user-selected rates: policy evaluation (*Soc Eval Inpt*), policy change ( *Soc Chnge Inpt*), new policy ( *Soc New Inpt* ), and policy term ination ( *Soc Term Inpt* ), respectively.

Corruption of the policy form ulation and im plementation processes takes p lace at a rate determined by the *Soc F&I Corrupt* parameter and corruption of the new policy tak es place at a rate determined by the *Soc CorrRte NewPol* parameter.

The control panel for the Social Policy Cycle Model, shown in Figure A6.2, perm its the user-selection of specific m odel parameter valu es, including social policy sensitivity (*Soc Pol Sensitiv*; set at 0.2), input rate to s ocial policy evaluation (*Soc Eval Input*; 0.1), input rate to social policy change (*Soc Chnge Input*; 0.1), input rate to social policy term ination (*Soc Term Input*; 0.1), input rate to new social policy (*Soc New Input*; 0.1), new social policy corruption rate (*Soc CorrRte NewPol* ; 0.04), and corruption rate of social policy form ulation and implementation (*Soc F&I Corrupt*; 0.04), for example.

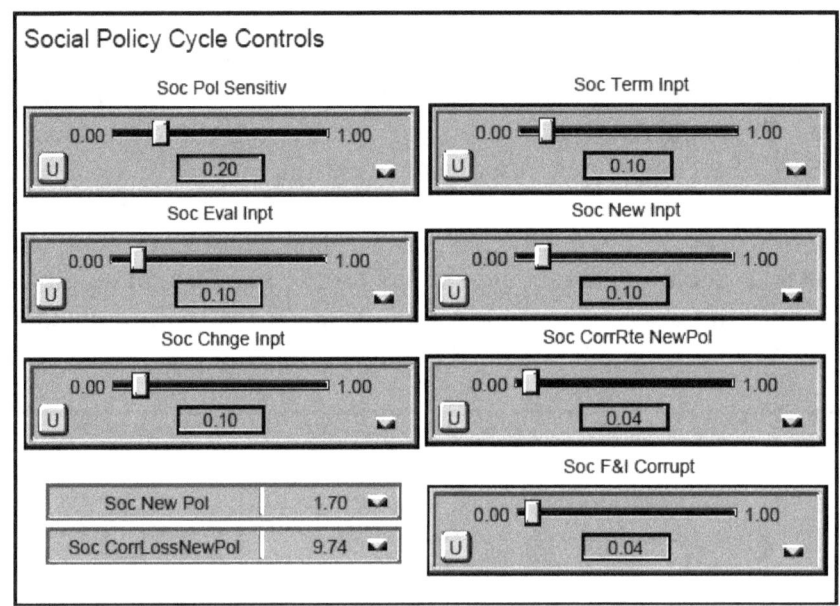

**Figure A6.2. Control panel for the Social Policy Cycle Model With Policy-Related Corruption.**

## A Security Policy Cycle Model

A *Security Policy Cycle Model* for the m anagement of entity security has been developed and implemented in systems dynamics software. Figure 24 presents the key features of the model and Figure A6.3 shows im plementation of the m odel in systems dynamics software. Input to the policy cycle model represents policy concerns relate d to the effect of casualty levels generated by notional terrorist actions that are made possible by lowered s ecurity threshold conditions and availability of trained terrorists. In the model terrorist actions trigger policy cycle-based actions assumed to represent the form ulation and im plementation of security p olicy that ar e aimed at increasing the level of entity security. Increased security can prevent terrorist events from taking place. Corruption with in the secu rity policy cy cle is assumed to reduce the ability of a government entity to increase security in response to increased amounts of terrorist activity.

Security-related policy cycle model activities involve the form ulation and implementation (*Sec F&I Tot*), evaluation (*Sec Eval Tot*), change (*Sec Change Tot*), new policy creation (*Sec New Pol*), and policy term ination (*Soc Term*) (Figure A6.3). These activities take place at user-

44

selected rates determined by user-selected security policy evaluation (*Sec Eval Inpt*), security policy change (*Sec Chnge Inpt*), new security policy (*Sec New Inpt*), and security policy termination (*Sec Term Inpt*) values, respectively.

Corruption of the policy formulation and implementation processes takes place at a rate determined by the (*Sec F&I Corrupt*) parameter and corruption of the new policy takes place at a rate determined by the (*Sec CorrRte NewPol*) parameter. Typical settings of the user-selectable parameters for the Security Policy Cycle Model control panel are shown in Figure A6.4.

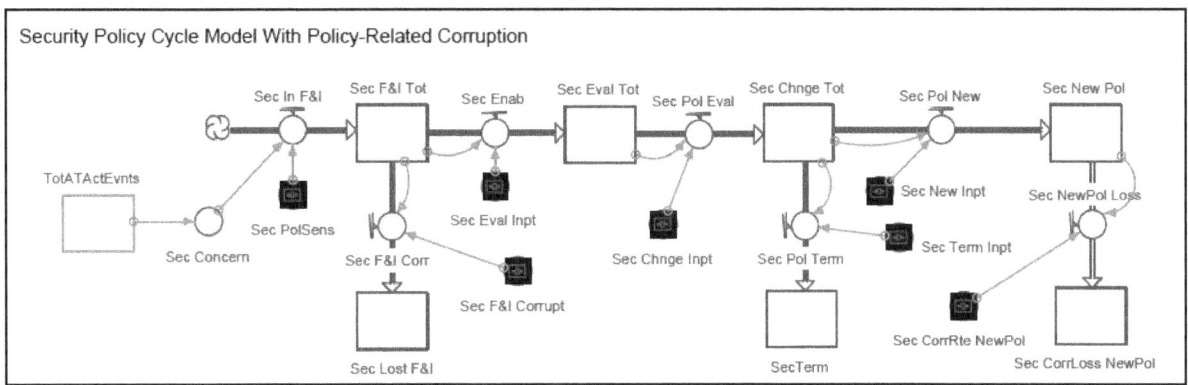

**Figure A6.3. Implementation of the Security Policy Cycle Model provides an environment for assessing the impact of the speed of policy cycle actions and the effect of policy-related corruption on the production of new policies and their effect on changing security levels and on the number of terrorist-related events and casualties.**

The control panel permits the user selection of specific model parameter values, including security policy sensitivity (*Sec Pol Sensitiv*; set at 0.2), input rate to security policy evaluation (*Sec Eval Input*; 0.1), input rate to security policy change (*Sec Chnge Input*; 0.1), input rate to security policy termination (*Sec Term Input*; 0.1), input rate to new security policy (*Soc New Input*; 0.1), new security policy corruption rate (*Sec CurrRte NewPol*; 0.1), and corruption rate of security policy formulation and implementation (*Sec F&I Corrupt*; 0.1).

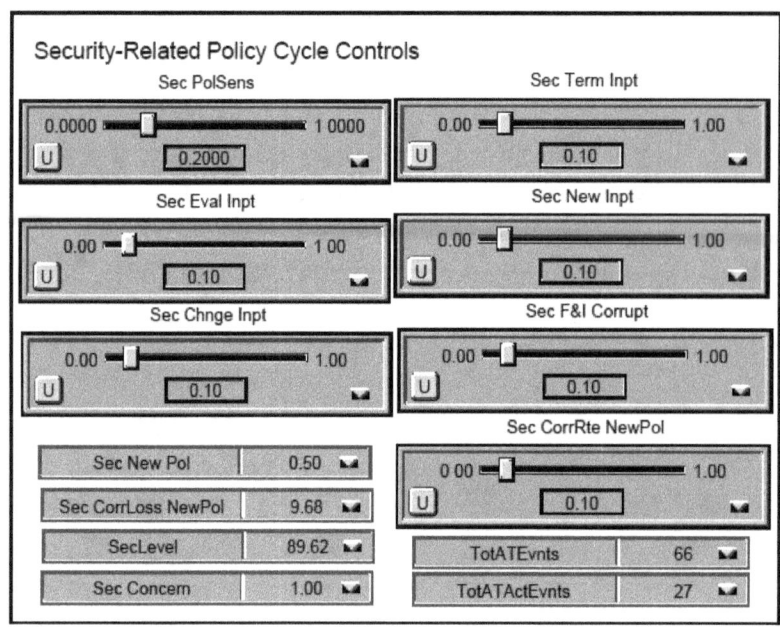

**Figure A6.4. Security Policy Cycle Model with policy-related corruption control panel. Settings indicate a sensitivity of 0.2 and policy cycle and corruption parameters of 0.1 (10 percent per time step).**

# REFERENCES

Davis David, Allison Frendak-Blu me, Tia W heeler, Clarence Worrell, and Ale xander E. R. Woodcock, 2003. Implementation of the Conceptual Model of Counter-Terrorist Operations (CMCTO) as a System s Dynamics Model: T echnical Report 1: The Conceptual Model of Counter-Terrorist Operations. Fairfax and Arlington, Virginia: George Mason University.

Lester, James P. and Joseph Stew art, Jr., 2000. *Public Policy: An E volutionary Approach*, Second Edition, Belmont, California: Wadsworth.

Woodcock, A. E. R., 2003. *Implementation of the Conceptual Model of Counter-Terrorist Operations (CMCTO) as a Systems Dynamics Model: Technical Report 2: the Systems Dynamics Model of C ounter-terrorist Operations.* Fairfax and Arlington, Virginia: George Mason University.

Woodcock, A. E. R., S. A. Christensson, and J. T. Dockery, 2009. *A Systemic A pproach is Needed for Fully-Integrated Civilian-Military Policy- and Decision-Making.* In: Woodcock, Alexander, George Rose, and David Davis (eds.) 2009, *Analysis in Support of Policy*. Arlington, Virginia, The Cornwallis Group. Access: http://www.thecornwallisgroup.org/pdf/ CXIII_9_WoodcockChristenssonDockery.pdf.

Woodcock Alexander and Allan F alconer, 2012. *Climate Change, Predator-Prey-Harvesting (PPH) and Policy Cycle Management (PCM) Models, and Sustainable Fisheries in Changing Supply Conditions. The International Journal of Climate Change: Im pacts and Responses.* Volume 3, Issue 1.

Woodcock, A. E. R. and L. Cobb, 1994. Count ernarcotics modeling and analysis. In: *Proceedings of the First Works hop on Command Information Systems*. Great Malvern: The Defence Research Agency.

Woodcock, A. E. R. a nd J. T. Dockery, 198 9. Models of com bat with em bedded C2 III: Recruitment, disaffection, and the tactic al control of insurgents. *International C.I.S. Journal* 3(1).